EDINBURGH

A Celebration

For David Graham,
who in 1969 adopted this city as his own
and enjoyed it to the full

EDINBURGH

A Celebration

MAINSTREAM
PUBLISHING

·BOWMAN·
ASSOCIATES
PARTNERSHIP

ACKNOWLEDGEMENTS

EDINBURGH - A Celebration *has been supported by a grant and pre-purchase by:*

LOTHIAN AND EDINBURGH ENTERPRISE LTD
THE CITY OF EDINBURGH DISTRICT COUNCIL
LOTHIAN REGIONAL COUNCIL
THE WESTER HAILES PARTNERSHIP

EDINBURGH - A Celebration *was devised by Michael Russell and Denis Robertson Sullivan.*

Design and Graphic Art was undertaken by Bowman Associates Partnership. Michael Chatfield was responsible for the Design and the Art Direction, assisted by Graham Davidson, Tracy Kydd and Mark Dawson. Editorial Assistance was provided by the staff of Ponsonby Sullivan Communications, particularly Graeme Cleugh.

Thanks are due to the following for helping in many different ways: Bill Campbell, Peter MacKenzie, Mike Ashton, Jane Cumming, David Hume, Sorrel Brookes, Cllr Devin Scobie, Alan Young, Ronnie Summers, Bill Simpson, Tracey Roney, Helen Crosthwaite, Paul Hunter, Iain Thorburn, Neil Hannay, David Sullivan, Edward Murray, Ian Brown, and Sheila Hamilton.

Thanks are also due to: David Patterson of the City Art Centre, Norma Armstrong of the Edinburgh Central Library, The National Galleries of Scotland, the Environment Centre, Drummond High School. Sean Hudson, the Daily Record and The Scotsman.

Additional photography was provided by Mark Dawson and Tracy Kydd.

First published in Great Britain in 1992 by
MAINSTREAM PUBLISHING COMPANY (EDINBURGH) LTD
7 Albany Street
Edinburgh EH1 3UG
and
BOWMAN ASSOCIATES PARTNERSHIP
The Old Church House, 102b Whitehouse Loan
Edinburgh EH9 1AX

ISBN 1 85158 517 6

A catalogue record for this book is available from the British Library.

Designed and typeset in 9 on 14pt Valencia Light by Bowman Associates Partnership. Origination by Interface Graphics, Edinburgh. Printed in Great Britain by Butler & Tanner Ltd, Frome, Somerset.

CONTENTS

Throughout the book there are images from a specially commissioned photo essay "Edinburgh" by Robert Pogson, which are highlighted with a yellow border.

ROBERT POGSON

Robert Pogson is an Edinburgh-based photographer working chiefly in advertising and editorial. He became interested in photography at sixteen, and through the encouragement of Alf Martin, the then editor of the Record Mirror, *went on to become a regular contributor to the music press. After leaving college he worked for six years as an illustrator, before finally returning to photography. During this period he travelled extensively in South America, the Himalayas and the Far East pursuing various photography projects.*

FOREWORD

THE RT. HON. IAN LANG MP,

Secretary of State for Scotland

Few cities in the world rank with Edinburgh in terms of history, beauty and quality of life for the people who live there.

That history and beauty, and her status as Scotland's capital, made Edinburgh the natural choice to host the meeting of the European Council, the culmination of the United Kingdom's Presidency of the European Community in 1992.

But Edinburgh is also a vibrant, modern city which is preparing itself for the challenges of the 21st century. In commerce, in the arts, in finance and in learning Edinburgh leads the way and others follow. In truth, Edinburgh is a city for all seasons.

Edinburgh nestles in a beautiful rolling landscape surrounded by the Pentland Hills and it is a gateway to the Scottish Borders. Its shoreline looks over to that of the Kingdom of Fife and they are joined by two magnificent bridges.

Visitors to Scotland seldom miss the opportunity to visit the capital. Few fail to be impressed by its myriad qualities. From the brooding presence of the volcanic Arthur's Seat to the elegant grandeur of the New Town, Edinburgh's beauty is multi-faceted indeed. When the sun shines, that beauty is breathtaking.

History seeps out of every one of Edinburgh's ancient closes and side streets. But the history is not moribund; it is alive. The Castle is still a barracks. The Palace of Holyrood House is still the official residence of the sovereign when in Scotland. And with the European Council in Edinburgh, history is still in the making.

The beauty and the history combine to offer the people of Edinburgh a remarkable quality of life. Fiercely, and rightly, proud of their city, Edinburgh's achievements are their achievements. The enterprise and initiative of her people have ensured that Edinburgh has always been at the centre of Scottish, British, European and world events, and she will remain so.

The many thousands of visitors who will come to Edinburgh will find a city well used to welcoming old friends and new. Her long and historic links with Europe made Edinburgh an especially appropriate city in which to stage a significant European gathering.

I hope that all of Edinburgh's visitors will take time to recognise the city's other distinctive features which mark her out as a city ready to grasp the opportunities which our ever-changing world provides.

Edinburgh is at the forefront of the financial services sector and is one of Europe's principal financial centres. With no fewer than three universities, the city is in the vanguard of the higher education revolution which is taking place in our country. And as home to one of the world's major arts festivals, the city is at the frontiers of artistic excellence.

So, Edinburgh has a great deal to offer. The Government, together with public sector agencies, local authorities, the private sector and individuals, is keen to work in a partnership to prepare Edinburgh for the problems and challenges that await. The example of working together to prepare for the European Council pointed that way ahead.

Edinburgh and Scotland have rightly basked in the European limelight of the European Council. But the lights will stay on. The Castle will still be standing for future generations to admire and the city will continue to go from strength to strength, an ever-greater source for pride in Scotland.

INTRODUCTION

MICHAEL RUSSELL

Why celebrate Edinburgh and the land in which it lies?

It is, after all, only one of several Scottish cities, all with distinctive characters and different strengths and weaknesses. Glasgow, larger than Edinburgh, is alive and vibrant. Its history of achievement in the nineteenth and early twentieth centuries is remarkable, and now it has risen above its more recent past of decline and decay. It has already been the European Capital of Culture and has invested determinedly in its own future.

Aberdeen is a granite masterpiece, cold and refreshing and rooted in the gritty northern culture of hard work and prosperity. It has successfully grafted on to its traditional industries the international culture of oil, and the mixture is a heady one.

Dundee is a working-class city with ambitions to attract a new type of incoming investment and tourism. It has brought home one of its great products - the exploration ship *Discovery* and attached to itself the tag of the "Discovery City". It wants to boldly go where no city in Scotland has gone before.

Perth calls itself the "Fair City" - but it is more than a county town with pretensions. And other towns in Scotland have ambitions to city status - Paisley has

a university, Stirling has a fine castle and Inverness a flourishing economy and two broadcasting bases.

But Edinburgh remains the capital of Scotland, although, in terms of money and power, Scotland really has two capitals: Edinburgh in the east and Glasgow in the west, joined by the umbilical cords of motorways and railway lines.

Edinburgh's capital city status rests firmly on history and tradition (and some would challenge it for that very reason!). But it still is the seat of government in Scotland - although that government lacks a Parliament. It is also a financial centre that rivals all others in Europe, with the exception of London. And it is undoubtedly the arts and publishing centre of Scotland - although broadcasting has adapted to demographic reality, and based itself in Glasgow.

Edinburgh is worth celebrating because it *is* the capital city and also because it has been more than a little overshadowed in recent years by the celebration of Glasgow, deserved as that is. But it is doubly worth celebrating Edinburgh and all its aspects at the end of 1992 because in December of that year the city formally re-entered the European political stage after decades, or centuries, of absence.

When the idea of a book to celebrate Edinburgh as a European city was first discussed Europe had not yet gone through the crisis of Maastricht or the turbulence of the ERM. But in the historical scheme of things these are minor matters. And to some extent, despite their domestic ramifications in terms of mortgages, loans and unemployment, they are also less than primary concerns for the ordinary citizens of this or any other city.

Day to day life in Edinburgh and its hinterland goes on despite the geopolitical forces that shape our destinies. This book celebrates that life.

It would be impossible in any book to detail everything that is of importance in any place. There will be those who will find something they wanted missing from this attempt - but overall it is to be hoped that the miscellany of opinion, facts and pictures will provide something new: something that allows the visitor or the resident to see into hidden corners and to appreciate aspects of the city that others may have missed.

EDINBURGH - A Celebration is designed to be a book to keep. A book that the reader can dip into today, or in twenty years time, and find something that may jog a memory or raise a forgotten experience to the surface of the mind. It is a book not for the coffee table, but for the much-consulted bookshelf, or the bedside, or wherever a minute or two can be found to browse. Those who were invited to contribute to the book had only one thing in common - they knew the city, or some aspect of the city, well. Their contributions are personal ones and the overall conception of the book is a personal one also - a view of the city and its people that relates to the personal experience of living and working there at some stage of their lives.

For everyone who comes here, or lives here, there are personal images that will be held and retained. For me they include childhood visits to my grandparents and to the printing works where my grandfather's office stood in what appeared to be vast, wood-panelled, cigar-smoked, dark-brown splendour. Today the site is occupied by a modern office block.

They include Arthur's Seat in the light of a snowy December night, and two hands clasped for the glowing timeless walk of new lovers; a terraced lecture hall and another pointless lecture; an office and a first job with a view of the Castle from the attic room; an early breakfast after a bitter political night without sleep; a friend and a funeral in the September sunshine. Each person who knows the city has memories as vivid as these are to me, and each person who visits the city rubs shoulders with those who hold such pictures in themselves.

But inevitably (and in time) these personal images are subsumed in the historical and contemporary facts that the city presents at every turn. These can be landscapes - the Castle, the hills of Lothian and the sea. These can be events and institutions: the Festivals, the City Council, the Court of Session, the Church, the universities. They can, of course, be people: people from history and literature such as Robert Louis Stevenson, David Hume, Allan Ramsay, Elsie Inglis, Mary of Guise, John Knox, Lord Cockburn and Robert Burns - or contemporary citizens such as some of those who have written for this book, or been written about.

This book has been supported by the City of Edinburgh District Council, Lothian Regional Council, Lothian and Edinburgh Enterprise Limited and by the Wester Hailes Partnership. Each of those bodies has responsibility for aspects of life in Edinburgh and each of them knows that a mere celebration of the city, no matter how wide-ranging or entertaining, is not enough. In order for the city to progress and grow it must do two things: acknowledge its past and present successes and failures, and creatively challenge its citizens to work for the future.

Edinburgh basks in the media spotlight not only during the Festival, but on other occasions during the year. At the European Summit it lent its historic palace and its new and old streets to be a backdrop for decision-making and a thousand pictures that will be seen throughout the world. That event can be part of the future as well as of the history, if those who live in Edinburgh and in other parts of Scotland choose to make it so. We can grasp now the benefits of trade and political progress within the wider European context, just as in the past we took such chances and built on them.

So as Edinburgh celebrates, and in this book records the things worth celebrating, it also remains in the tide of progress and will steer itself back into the European mainstream for the twenty-first century. Edinburgh knows where it has been. It also knows where it's going.

Edinburgh is a city worth celebrating at any time. But it is now at a point of time worth celebrating also. This book sets out to do both - and also to state one further truth.

For the visitor and for the resident Edinburgh can and always will be a personal celebration.

'When standing at the 'Giant's Ribs', on the south side of Arthur's Seat, I felt as if one of the grandest pages of the earth's history lay open before me'

JAMES NASMYTH

THE EUROPEAN COUNCIL

A message from
THE RT. HON.
BRUCE MILLAN,
Commissioner of the
European Community

The holding in Edinburgh of the European Council's meeting during the United Kingdom's Presidency of the Council of Ministers is a new and important event to add to the rich history of the city. The decision to hold the Council meeting in Edinburgh was a recognition of its status as capital of Scotland and a reflection of the city's growing European and international vocation.

My present responsibilities in Brussels as European Commissioner for Regional Policy have allowed me to travel extensively throughout Europe visiting many regions and cities in the Member States. I can therefore testify that Edinburgh stands comparison as a modern dynamic centre of enterprise and culture with Europe's other leading cities.

Edinburgh is characterised by the rare diversity of the roles it plays: as a historical capital city; as a political and administrative centre of government; as an important domestic and international financial and commercial centre; as a city with respected universities and seats of learning; as a city of culture hosting one of Europe's most important and varied annual festivals; as home of some of the most visited museums and art galleries in Britain; and as one of Britain's most important tourist centres, earning considerable amounts of foreign currency for the UK economy.

Although geographically near to the periphery of Europe, Edinburgh draws on its many attributes to be very much at the heart of the Community. This is in line with a long involvement of Scottish intellectual life with continental Europe.

Many important international companies recognise the city's advantages by locating in and around Edinburgh. A convenient international airport on its doorstep helps and in a few years Edinburgh should be able to draw benefit from the opening of the Channel Tunnel.

To succeed in the modern world, cities need to develop and modernise in a way which produces sustainable economic growth and not a congested, polluted environment. Edinburgh has experience in these matters. The "New Town" was an exercise in town planning which continues to excite admiration two centuries after its inception. That Edinburgh maintains its reputation as a city offering a high quality of life reflects the fact that careful planning has brought modernisation without destroying the historical heritage. Although the city as such is not eligible for regional assistance, the Community has assisted in the financing of the ring-road around Edinburgh which has done so much to relieve the city centre of through-traffic.

Edinburgh can look forward to a bright future in an enlarged European Community in the new century. The Heads of State and Government attending the European Council and the tens of thousands of other visitors through the years are able to see for themselves a city proud of its past and confident of its future.

Bruce Millan

A EUROPEAN CITY

BILLY KAY

Billy Kay is a writer and broadcaster of radio and television programmes which specialise in Scottish language, history and culture and examine their place within the context of European culture. His books include *Scots The Mither Tongue* and *Knee Deep in Claret*. He has written plays for radio and the stage, while four of his radio documentaries have won international awards.

EDINBURGH
1992

'Like the majority of people in this stunningly beautiful capital of ours, I feel thoroughly Scots, thoroughly European, and proud of being both'

The neoclassical splendour of her late 18th century New Town reinvents the elegance and symmetry of ancient Greece, a physical symbol of her intellectual claim to be the New Athens of the modern age. In the romantic chaos of her Auld Toun, the tall lands and crow stepped gables recall her trade with Flanders, while streets like the Vennel or the West Port provide a link with her early French inhabitants. At the turn of our present century, the Grassmarket at the foot of the Castle attracted the majority of her sizeable Italian community, because it reminded them of the piazza at home.

Edinburgh's looks are imbued with the culture of continental Europe. So at one time was her way of life. A visitor in 1661, Jorevin de Rocheford wrote: *"In the best houses they dress their victuals after the French method"*. The wines available at the Scottish court at Holyrood included those of the Rhine, Burgundy, the Loire and Bordeaux, while the Edinburgh diary of the writer and bon vivant, James Boswell in March 1775 recalls *"an easy, genteel dinner. We had two kinds of Greek wine, Port, Madeira, Mountain, Claret"*. Bozzie was obviously a good European - drinking a wine from almost every country in the community at one sitting! But the connections were not merely of the sensual variety. Duns Scotus and George Buchanan were two Scottish thinkers of European stature. The tomb of Duns Scotus at Cologne states: *Scotia me genuit, Anglia suscepit, Gallia edocuit, Germania tenet*. In the later 16th century Buchanan influenced the philosopher Montaigne at Bordeaux, then taught at the University of Coimbra in Portugal before returning to tutor the infant King James VI in Edinburgh. He also found time to correspond with the Danish astronomer Tycho Brahe.

'...in the gentle mildness of summers the evening sun has shone upon thy verdant sides diversified with rugged moss-clad rocks'

JAMES BOSWELL

Prince Charles Edward Stuart in Edinburgh, 1745. *William Brassey Hole (City Art Centre, Edinburgh)*

As we shall see, the Scots language spoken then (and surviving still along with Gaelic and English in this multilingual country) gives living testimony to the profoundly European nature of Scottish culture. *Edinburgh, Edimbourg, Edimburgo* - is it a remote provincial British city or a dynamic capital and pivotal cultural centre of the new Europe? If its citizens need help in choosing the future role for their city they need look no further for inspiration than their own history.

The precocious Scottish sense of national identity forged at least as early as the 12th century, is all the more remarkable when you consider the disparate groups who inhabited the country. The polyglot nature of the early Scottish kingdom is confirmed in the royal charters of the period addressed to, *Francis et Anglis, Scotis et Flemmingis* - Norman French, Northern English, Scots and Flemish. The French and Flemish were the first of many European peoples to be absorbed into the melting pot of Scottish culture. The origins of the Auld Alliance between France and Scotland lie in myth and legend - Charlemagne is supposed to have sent an envoy suggesting military co-operation as early as the year 777 - but the first formal treaty was between Philippe le Bel and John Balliol in 1295, at the beginnlng of the Wars of Independence against England. The great historian Froissart accompanied a force of 2,000 Frenchmen to support Scotland in the reign of Robert II. From then through to the Reformation in the middle of the 16th century, French troops were frequently stationed in Scotland, and Scots soldiers formed the backbone of the forces which eventually removed the English occupiers from French soil. Their elite formed *La Garde Ecossaise du Corps du Roi* - the Scots Guard regiment - the personal bodyguard to French kings from then through to the 19th century, by which time it was Scots only in name. The Scots had a formidable military reputation in France; a l6th-century chronicler wrote, *"Ils aiment mieux mourir pour honneur garder, que vivre en honte, reprochez de tasche de laschete"* - "they prefer to die with honour, rather than live in shame, reproached with the stain of cowardice". Out of that reputation, came the old French proverb, *Fier comme un Ecossais* - Proud as a Scot.

The cultural influence of the Auld Alliance was profound, especially in its heyday when Marie de Guise and her daughter Mary Queen of Scots presided over the Court in Edinburgh. In 1513 both countries granted joint French and Scottish citizenship to their people. The prestige of the French language, coupled with the earlier influence of Norman French meant that the Scots language was *spairged* (fr asperger, to sprinkle) with French words; *jigot* (lamb), *ashet* (deep dish), *douce* (soft or sweet), *to fash* (bother) and *disjune* (breakfast). The poet Pierre de Ronsard visited Scotland and composed a poem praising James V on the occasion of his marriage to Madeleine de Valois. French architects and masons modelled the palaces of Falkland, Linlithgow, Stirling and Holyrood on the chateaux of the Loire. Trade between the two countries flourished, with wine so important it was christened "the bloodstream of the Auld Alliance." Knowing our partiality for drink, in fact, a cynic could interpret the whole Scottish involvement in the campaigns against the English as an attempt to get hold of the wine trade. Bordeaux was an

David Hume

'We only came for a day and a day just isn't enough! The whole city is beautiful, especially the architecture'

MRS LESLEY HOSKIN
& HUSBAND
CORNWALL

*'The spectacle
of the old Town,
seen from the new,
is inspiring and
splendid, and places
Edinburgh, from the
artistic point of view,
on a level with
Constantinople
and Stockholm'*

JOHN RUSKIN

English colony, but when the English were removed, Scots grabbed the initiative and as allies gained certain economic and practical privileges. These allowed Scotsmen to get the pick of each vintage and have it home for Hogmonay, which incidentally is another word we got from the French, *Aguillaneuf!* The Scots priviliges in the wine trade lasted until Colbert (a Frenchman of Scots descent) withdrew them. Even after the Union beween Scotland and her auld enemy England, the Scots continued to drink claret as it became a symbol of resistance to the English and their port drinking traditions: the epigram by John Home sums it up:

"Firm and erect the Caledonian stood

Old was his mutton and his claret good

'Let them drink port' the English statesman cried.

He drank the poison and his spirit died!"

Gey few spirits died; they simply smuggled the claret in and continued drinking it in great quantities. There is still a strong claret drinking and appreciating tradition in Scotland that stems from those days, and is being strengthened by the return to popularity of wine drinking. Culturally too, the links are maintained, with at least five recent translations into Scots of Moliere's works appearing in Edinburgh's theatres, and a Scot, Kenneth White, established as one of France's most influential poets.

If France's influence was cultural, Flanders led the way in industry, trade and commerce. Flemish people have been trading with Scotland and settling in her towns from the 11th century onwards. When David I founded royal burghs all over his realm, he made sure they were stocked with Flemish people. With its fine weaving trade, Flanders was more advanced industrially than most parts of Europe and it led the way in the organisation of crafts and trade within its cities. Scottish merchants established a Staple in several Flemish towns such as Middleburg, Antwerp, and Bruges before settling in Campveere in Zeeland. The Staple was a little Scotland planted on foreign soil in Europe's most advanced mercantile area.

Part social, part commercial centre, it looked after an extensive trade right through the middle ages - Scots hides, wool, fish, skins, and eventually coal and salt being imported in return for fine Flemish cloth, soap, spices, fruit and onions, furniture and luxury goods. The distinctive Dutch red pantiles were also carried as ballast on the ships coming home, and the results can be seen in the traditional architecture of the coastal villages around Edinburgh.

Flemish weavers brought their skins and advanced the Scots ability to manufacture their abundance of raw materials. Common Scots surnames like Fleming, Bremner (from Brabanter,) and Wyper (from Ypres) all tell of their forebears' place of origin in Flanders. There was so much trade and personal contact with Scots and Flemish, that Flemish words also became established in the Scots tongue; *pinkie, golf, scone, howff* are in everyday use all over the country, while others survive in certain dialects; to *redd* (tidy up), *loun* (boy), *hunkers* (haunches) and *doited* (daft). Scottish soldiers played a crucial role in Dutch history too: particularly in the revolts against Spanish rule in the Northern Provinces which

'It's very nice, I'd like to see everything'

LEOPOLDO COPPOLA
ITALY

'I've enjoyed seeing all Edinburgh's historic places, but I especially liked walking down Princes Street again'

MRS M McLAREN
& HUSBAND
BLACKPOOL

'I like this city. There is nowhere like it in Japan'

MASANORI TADOKORO
& WIFE
LONDON

resulted in Dutch independence. In that struggle, the Scots Brigade was in the thick of the action on the Dutch side in the early 1590s. After the wars many soldiers never returned to Scotland, and became Dutch citizens. As late as the 18th century Rotterdam had a Scottish population numbering over a thousand.

Probably the greatest debt we Scots owe the Dutch, however, is in the development of our legal system. Both Dutch and Scots Law are derived from Roman civil law, so the universities of Leyden, Utrecht, Franeker and Groningen attracted many Scots students. Some were studying law as early as 1430 but the great century was between 1650 and 1750. Of the 100 plus Scots students attending Leyden in the late 17th century, over half studied law. The man known as the father of Scots law, James Dalrymple, Viscount Stair arrived as a political refugee in Holland in 1682 and remained at the university of Leyden until 1688, before taking what he had learned back to Scotland.

Another major group of settlers in old Edinburgh originated in the area of Northern England called the Danelaw, and they brought their language with them. Many of the features which distinguish modern Scots from Standard English came as a result of this Danish legacy; *kirk*, *kist* and *breeks* for church, chest and breeches; *brig* and *rig* for bridge and ridge. Trade between the East of Scotland and the Baltic was intensive, and as you had to go through the Sound of Jutland to reach the Baltic, the Scots literally set up shop in Danish ports like Elsinore and Aalborg. The trade alliance went back to the marriage between James I and Princess Margaret of Denmark in 1469, but the heyday of Scottish enterprise in

*'I do wonder
that so brave
a prince
as King James
should be borne in
so stinking a toun
as Edinburgh
in lousy
Scotland'*

SIR ANTHONY WELDON

Denmark was the late 16th century when Scots rose to such prominence in the ports of the Sound that Alexander Lyall became mayor of Elsinore while David Paterson was mayor of Malmo, over in Sweden.

The business and cultural ties were strengthened by James VI's marriage to Anne of Denmark. James spent a winter in Norway and Denmark (then under the same crown) when he married Anne. Anne was a popular queen, despite her reputation for spending many of Jamie's scarce shillings on clothes and jewellery. Danish noblemen settled in Scotland as part of her retinue and their court in Edinburgh was a centre for poets, musicians and intellectuals. Danish students flocked to the Scottish universities, and when the University of Copenhagen was founded it had Scots professors of Medicine and Divinity. Trade between Scotland and Germany was firmly established by 1297. In that year, we have a letter from the patriot leader William Wallace to the Senate of Lubeck advising them that he had removed the English army of occupation, so they should inform their merchants *"that they now can have safe access with their merchandise to all harbours of the Kingdom of Scotland"*. By the early 1400s German factors were established in Edinburgh, to sell their countrymen's goods within Scotland, while Danzig was a haven for Scots merchants. From around 1380 there was an established Scots quarter of the town, called *Alt Schottland*, originally of weavers and tanners, but eventually home to merchants as well By the 17th century so many Scots boys had flocked to Danzig to seek their fortune, that the Scottish consul Patrick Gordon issued an edict to prevent more travelling there - they were becoming a nuisance and an embarrassment to the wealthier Scots community. Many became itinerant peddlers in East and West Prussia in the hinterland of the Baltic ports which was a mosaic of German and Polish speaking areas. With more than 20,000 Scots actively involved in trade there throughout the century, it is little

Gillies MacBain at Culloden.
L. Dickinson after R. R. McIan.
(City Art Centre, Edinburgh)

'I'm sorry
to report the
Scott Monument
a failure. It is like
the spire of a
Gothic church
taken off
and stuck in
the ground'

CHARLES DICKENS

The Signing of the National Covenant. *Sir William Allan (City Art Centre, Edinburgh)*

A SNAPSHOT OF EDINBURGH

Laura Fiorentini

It was love at first sight. Arriving in Edinburgh, back in 1980, looking from Soutra Hill down at the city skyline in the amazing light of a clear summer dawn, the impression was of total astonishment and fulfilment. I was 'coming home' at last to the place I always belonged in my dreams and from the first moment it was as if I have been living here all my life. The great enthusiasm and the sheer pleasure of living in this marvellous city have not faded away with the years, and, to this day, they are for me as strong and as deep as ever.

It is difficult to explain why Edinburgh is so congenial to my character, what I like here that I cannot find elsewhere, not even, I would say, in my own native country. There is the striking architecture; there are the wonderful diverse colours of a typically northern latitude, rapidly changing skies, golden summer sunsets, the intense brilliance of the winter light. But, above all, there is the enjoyment of everyday life. To my mind, Edinburgh is the perfect place for a civilised existence: its compact size means you can live and work here without losing your individuality, as would happen in the anonymity, stress and chaos of a modern, larger metropolis. Although I work in a predominantly Italian environment, I have made a great many Scottish friends as well. I think Italians feel particularly at home here, because of the friendliness of the people and because they recognise in Edinburgh a capital with deep European roots in every aspect of its character.

'It's very different, the weather most of all'

CHIARA LINO
ITALY

surprise that the word schotte meant both Scot and peddler in the German language. A German historian summed up their legacy: *"The increase in strength and industrial capacity which this Scottish admixture instilled into the German was of the very highest importance, and it can scarcely be doubted that the peculiar compound of stubbornness and shrewdness which characterises the inhabitants of the small towns of Eastern Prussia has its root in the natural disposition of the Scot."*

The Scottish cultural links with Germany are long standing and fascinating. Gaelic-speaking monks spread christianity there in the 6th and 7th centuries and founded the *Schottenkloster* - the Scots monasteries famous for their teaching. St James at Ratisbon was still a thoroughly Scottish staffed institution as late as the 17th century, with the catholic martyr St John Ogilvie one of many famous Scots who studied there.

At the end of the 18th century and the beginning of the 19th century, the cult of the noble savage, of folk poetry, and the rise of the Romantic Movement made Scotland a place of pilgrimage for German artists and intellectuals. They dreamed of *die blaue Ferne* - the hazy blue yonder - where man was simpler and in tune with nature. Sir Walter Scott's romantic poetry and novels and the widespread success of James Macpherson's *Ossian* led to Scotland providing Germany with the perfect romantic landscape. They came in their hundreds; Scott had already translated Goethe into English and the compliment was reciprocated later on when the German novelist Theodor Fontane translated Burns and the Border Ballads into German. Other arts were affected too, with the composer

THE EDINBURGH EUROPEAN SUMMIT

In May 1991, the Prime Minister, John Major announced the choice of Edinburgh as the host city for what is fast becoming one of the most important European Summit meetings in the history of the European Community. The United Kingdom holds the Presidency of the Community from July 1992 until December 1992.

The European Summit, being held on 11 and 12 December, will be the culmination of the British Government's presidency. This summit meeting will involve the Heads of Government from all twelve member states, coming together to discuss issues vital to the future of the Community.

The Summit will take place at the Palace of Holyrood House, scene of many a famous political event in the history of Scotland. There will also be a Ministerial lunch at Edinburgh Castle and a dinner on the Royal Yacht *Britannia*, in the presence of Her Majesty The Queen.

The arrangements for the Summit have to be extensive. The Palace is being carefully converted to accommodate the large number of delegates from the governments of member states and from the

Mendelssohn inspired to compose his overture known now as *'The Hebrides'*. This German interest in Scottish culture continues today. The University of Mainz at Germersheim has a department of Scottish Studies, while other German universities teach Scottish literature and language.

Of all the peoples of the European Community today, the Scots have probably had most contact with the Italians. Every Scottish town has a small Italian community due to waves of migration here from Tuscany and the Abruzzi in the late 19th century. The catering trade was their principal employment, and they established the Scottish taste for ice cream and fish and chips in their cafés! Through mutual aid within the community, many gained prosperity; between 1911 and 1931 Italian-owned cafés and restaurants in Scotland increased from 278 to 700. The descendants of the original immigrants are now in every profession in Scotland, while people like Tom Conti, Emilio Coia, Marcella Evaristi and Richard Demarco have played an exceptional role in Edinburgh's artistic life. Most Scots Italians nowadays are probably more Scottish than Italian - except in the one crucial area of football. There they continue supporting the Azzuri rather than the boys in dark blue.

Before the 19th-century immigration, and ignoring the considerable effect of the Roman occupation of southern Scotland, the main Italian influence has been on the literary and artistic plane. In the 13th century the great university for the study of Law, Bologna, attracted many Scots students, Later, at the time of the Rennaissance, Humanist teaching reached Scotland via the Italian universities. Italian writers such as Boccaccio and Ariosto influenced medieval Scottish

'Edinburgh is a grand European city, one of the beads that make up beautiful Europe'

*ECUART GREEN
GERMANY*

Commission. The conference facilities will include interpreting booths, 13 sets of offices and other rooms for the translation and production of documents. Space is needed for between 600 and 800 people.

And of course media from all over the world will be coming to Edinburgh to cover the Summit for their newspapers, radio and TV stations. Meadowbank Sports Centre will be converted into a fully equipped media centre for the 2,500 accredited press. For these two days, Edinburgh will be the focus for Europe and the world. This opportunity for the city has not

been lost on Edinburgh's civic leaders who are planning a programme of events to coincide with the Summit - arts events, exhibitions, displays, and a lot more.

John Major will chair the Summit meetings with Douglas Hurd at his side. President Mitterand of France, Chancellor Khol of Germany and all the other European leaders will be there. This will be a Summit on which the entire future of the Community depends. As the first full post-Maastricht Summit, it will go down as a turning point for the Community.

'The castle and the galleries are wonderful; I like the food, I love beer in pubs; I like to shop. I enjoy the whole experience'

NORMA BISHOP
CANADA

literature. King James IV and King James VI had Italian musicians and minstrels at Court and of course Mary Queen of Scots had her unfortunate favourite in David Rizzio. In the 18th century, the vogue for Italian music and musicians was such that defenders of the native tradition like the poet Robert Fergusson felt threatened by it. A *"bastard breed"* is his dismissive term for the Edimbourgeois who were deserting Scots song in favour of Italian music. The great tenor voice in Edinburgh in the 1770s, was Giusto Ferdinando Tenducci but he was not alone. A contemporary writer claimed *"every girl in Edinburgh who plays the pianoforte learns Italian, and Italian masters are to be found in every street."*

It was not just the music: Italian fashion was popular - in another poem Ferguson denigrates the dandies who follow the latest Milan styles as "macaronies". The taste for Italian style of course has never waned, and if you can afford an Armani suit, you might still be the object of a few jealous comments! Rome and Florence were the principal destinations of the scores of Scottish aristocrats, plus painters like Allan Ramsay and architects like Robert Adam who travelled Europe in the age of the Grand Tour. Their artistic embellishment of Edinburgh was undoubtedly influenced by their sojourns in Italy.

View of Edinburgh, 1759. *William Delacour (City Art Centre, Edinburgh)*

As the principal Catholic power in Europe at the time of the Protestant Reformation, the Spanish influence in Edinburgh tended towards helping the pro-catholic factions in Scottish politics attempt to regain the country for Catholicism. Obviously that never happened but the policy had some fascinating consequences, including the creation of a seminary for the training of priests - the *Colegio Real de Escoceces* in Madrid, then Valladolid, and now Salamanca. It was founded in 1627 by Colonel William Semple. The extreme religious climate of the time can be gauged by an attempt by the Edinburgh Presbytery to prevent Scots merchants travelling to Spain for wine because of *"danger for their saulis"*. When the merchants pointed out that they would be unable to recover bad debts if prevented from travelling, the presbytery relented; saving souls was not to get in the way of making money!

Spain continued to try and help the Catholic faction in Scottish politics right through till the Jacobite rebellions of the 18th century: indeed there was a

SNAPSHOT OF EDINBURGH

Werner Kittel

Upon arrival in Scotland I was
informed by a Glaswegian that if I
broke a leg in Princes Street people
would just keep walking past. Eleven
years on, limbs thankfully intact, I still
live in Scotland's capital. Most of the
credit for that goes to the people I
have met here, not only natives but
also the many incomers from south of
the border for whom Edinburgh has
become home.

For me the choice of this damp
and windy and overpriced city as
permanent place of residence is
largely down to physical attraction.
A painfully long winter, the general
lack of sunshine and low
temperatures is offset by the
experience of running through the
Braid Hills in spring, the air heavy
with the scent of gorse; those
glorious views of Arthur's Seat and
the Castle; breathtaking vistas across
the Forth to Fife.

If living slap-bang in the centre
of a cultural capital gets too much
there is always an escape route to the
Highlands. It brings me great pleasure
to be on the doorstep of one of
Europe's last wildernesses.

mini Spanish invasion supporting the Jacobite cause which reached the Highlands via a landing in Stornoway in 1718. It was put down fairly easily.

But whilst prepared to support the Catholic re-conquest of Scotland, Spain was certainly not prepared to see a Protestant country like Scotland establish a colony in its own Central American sphere of influence. This is what happened in the 1690s when "New Caledonia", the Scottish colony in Darien in the Isthmus of Panama, was planted. Weakened by disease and awaiting supply ships, the colonists managed to beat back the Spanish forces ranged against them at the little known battle of Toubacanti. Eventually though they were worn down and were given honourable terms of surrender provided they abandoned the colony. This they did, though the remains of Fort St Andrew and the houses of New Edinburgh are still to be found in the jungle of Darien. Before news of the loss of the colony reached Edinburgh, a medal was struck to commemorate the heroes of Toubacanti. However, in the 18th century many Scots Jacobites were exiled in Spain, and

'...Under these trees walked, and talked, and meditated, all our literary and scientific, and many of our legal worthies'

LORD COCKBURN

Lord Cockburn

settled in Cadiz and Jerez, where they entered the sherry trade. Duff Gordon was one of the early Scots firms there, and there are Spanish speaking Mackenzies still in the trade today.

Wine also provides the principal link between Edinburgh and Portugal. Following the Union in 1707, England's foreign markets were opened up to the Scots, and they had a huge influence on the Madeira and port trade. The experiments to fortify the wines with brandy were carried out by Francis Newton, a Fifer, in Madeira and in Oporto by George Sandeman from the fair city of Perth. In the world of port, the shippers' names even today read like a Scottish football team - Robertson, Graham, Tait, Dow, Mackenzie, Campbell Menzies, Sandeman and Cockburn.

Sandeman and Cockburn are of course two of the greatest names still with a strong presence in Oporto and the Douro. Cockburns began in Edinburgh, and you can see the family name above two of the finest wine shops in the city centre. In 1826, Archibald Cockburn wrote home to his sister in Edinburgh for a *"copy of the Scotch minstrel. They have one set of Scotch Quadrilles here, but very poor"*. Scottish country dancing was obviously in vogue in Oporto's beautiful Factory House whose Georgian elegance could have been designed by Robert Adam and would not look out of place in Edinburgh's New Town.

But is this just another nostalgic Scot singing of Auld Lang Syne and past glories that will never return? Is contemporary Edinburgh content to be international and European for only two days in December 1992? I think not. The song *Auld Lang Syne* is an example of something intensely Scots, yet which is translated and sung by millions in every language in Europe. Like Burns's song we can be both Scottish and universal.

There is a tremendous revival in Scottish culture going on presently. While in the recent past we looked over our shoulder to England as a cultural model, we now have the growing confidence to celebrate our own unique cultural contribution to Europe. We see the advances made by similar ancient nations like Catalonia, and feel that the Europe of a Hundred Flags rather than of the outmoded nation states may be where our future lies.

Most Scots feel at one with their European identity. David Hume recognised Paris rather than London as Edinburgh's equal during the period of the Scottish Enlightenment. His affinities are shared by many today, including this writer. When my book *Scots: The Mither Tongue* was published I was invited to speak on the subject at five ancient German universities. I am godfather to a little French boy called Johnston, whose family of *negociants* have been in the Bordeaux area since they settled there from Scotland in the 18th century. My wife is Portuguese, and my summers are spent speaking that language on a quinta in the foothills of the Serra da Estrela. Like the majority of people in this stunningly beautiful capital of ours, I feel thoroughly Scots, thoroughly European, and proud of being both.

'The first thing I saw when I jumped out of the train was nice buildings - so many of them'

CLAUDE SAUER
WEST GERMANY

'When I look out in the morning it is as if I had waked up in Utopia'

GEORGE ELLIOT

'I like the way the city is laid out and the people are very friendly'

ANGELA JONES
AUSTRALIA

*'The haughty
Dun-Edin,
the Queen
of the North'*

JAMES HOGG

The State Entry of Queen Mary into Edinburgh, 1561. *Inset:* Queen Mary brought captive to Edinburgh
William Brassey Hole (City Art Centre, Edinburgh)

THE CITY
AND
THE COUNTRY

CHARLES McKEAN

Charles McKean is Secretary, Treasurer
and Chief Executive of the Royal Incorporation
of Architects in Scotland and a notable writer
and authority on architecture.
He is the author of the acclaimed
Edinburgh - Portrait of a City.

*'The essence of
civilised life, those
habits of intimacy and
intellectual exchange,
could revive in
Edinburgh...'*

In the beginning was the winged camp, on its volcanic plug overlooking the flood plains of the Forth. Nicknamed *Castle of the Maidens,* probably after a shrine to Morgain la Fee (evil genius of Arthurian legend), and then after St Margaret, it became a citadel, and spawned a town on the upper part of its rock. Down by the estuary of the Water of Leith, there grew a port: a port that became Scotland's principal one and - up to 1603 - the country's main point of entry from abroad. The burgeoning European and Baltic mercantile success of Leith traders became the mercantile success of Edinburgh.

Edinburgh was a city without streets: just Europe's largest market-place - over one hundred feet broad and over half a mile long, like a gigantic egg-timer. It was pinched in the middle by the Burgh Kirk (with its craft aisles and chapels) in an island of shops and houses. The walls of this stone trough rose gradually to an average of six storeys to the street (attracting the admiration of all visitors) with up to fourteen storeys behind. The town had little need of a city wall: access from the west was up a steep, narrow and tortuous path known as the West Bow and military invasion was almost impossible through the tight narrow closes which sieved any army into single file. The city's one great gate - the Netherbow - stood like a mute in the trumpet, facing east towards the auld enemy of England. Not that the auld enemy ever gave up trying. Edinburgh was besieged, invaded or endured attempted sack some seventeen times - one of the most grievous records in European history, and in 1544, King Henry VIII left nobody in any doubt as to what should be done: *"His Majesty's pleasure is that you shall . . . out all to fire and sword, burn Edinburgh town, so razed and defaced when you have sacked and gotten what you can of it, that there may remain forever a perpetual memory of the vengeance of God . . . burn and subvert all the rest, putting man, woman and child to fire and sword without exception."*

'...how can I forget the glory of that scene on the still nights in which I have stood in Queen Street or the opening of the north-west corner of Charlotte Square...'

LORD COCKBURN

The Old Town of Edinburgh matured between 1580 and 1637, and the period of its greatest mercantile prosperity combined with its role as a major European capital city. It is the husk of that city that we know today.

After Scottish Kings had adopted Holyrood Abbey as the principal Royal seat, Edinburgh had to broaden from merely mercantile matters. The upside was that the court and its associated wealth now had a permanent seat in Edinburgh. But there was no space left facing the High Street: so courtiers and nobles either built at the bottom end of the closes (where you will find Lady Stair's House, for example), down in the Canongate suburb, or in villas built in the pleasant countryside beyond. King Charles elevated St Giles to cathedral status in 1633, for a brief period, and turned its graveyard over to the construction of the Parliament House of Scotland. But St Giles remained a mercantile kirk, and for State occasions they had to borrow the grandeur of suburban Holyrood Abbey where, by now, Scotland's monarchs had created a palace of unusual splendour. The fact is that Edinburgh had become a capital too late to garner the palaces, cathedrals, stately squares and piazzas that so adorn other capital cities.

However, 17th-century wealth brought money and buildings as the mercantile princes - the Fuggers of Edinburgh - like Sir William Dick of Braid with his bank in London and agents in Paris brought in the goods. The tenements facing the High Street were rebuilt in fine stonework and given vividly painted interiors sitting upon arcades as was the norm in Europe just like Salzburg or Chiavari. The expanding population required two new churches, villas proliferated, the King built a new palace within the Castle, the University expanded into a double courtyard (just like Glasgow), and the city's charitable endeavours were increased immeasurably by the arrival of George Heriot's Hospital. Traces of all this remain if you care to search them out.

The wars from 1637, late 17th-century depression, and the collapse of the Darien Scheme had the principal effect of consigning Edinburgh's great merchants to history (the mantle being picked up by Glasgow). Sir William Dick died in a debtors' prison in 1655. Edinburgh's future lay elsewhere: and from being a capital city, and a great mercantile emporium, it became a capital of the intellect.

Most European capital cities had continued to develop and expand between 1630 and 1730, subject to politics, economy and war; Edinburgh remained frozen, and the Canongate went into severe decline after the departure of Parliament to London in 1707. Yet the city remained the focus of two national institutions - the Scots Law, and the Scots Kirk - and soon developed a further specialism (as part of a deliberate marketing policy by the City fathers) in Scots Medicine. Upon these three foundations was constructed the Enlightenment. Density in the Old Town of Edinburgh could rise to as much as 700 people per acre: all classes were promiscuously intermingled (with a consequence for both literature and philosophy that marked it utterly separate from London), and for eight months in the year, the intelligentsia benefited from the inescapable meeting of people with people. For the four months of the year of the legal recess, they

Allan Ramsay's House, High Street. *The Cavaye collection of Thomas Begbie prints (City Art Centre, Edinburgh)*

'The City is built between two steep hills and the Castle on another, so that it may not improperly be compar'd to a spread Eagle'

JOSEPH TAYLOR

*'The view
of Edinburgh
from the road
before you enter
Leith is quite
enchanting:
it is, as Albert said,
"fairy-like"'*

QUEEN VICTORIA

ENVIRONS AND THE ENVIRONMENT

Gordon Greenhill

retired to isolation in their rustic villas for the purposes of contemplation and fresh air. Edinburgh became a city-scaled university, its cloister the arcaded High Street, its college gates the Netherbow gates which were *girt struck* each evening at ten o'clock, its debating chambers the streets, clubs and howffs. A distinguishing feature of Edinburgh's Enlightenment was its requirement for those at the forefront of their discipline to communicate across disciplines, usually in the media of the clubs. That more than anything else was what created in Scotland an intellectual aristocracy. The density and the absence of politicians and aristocrats encouraged an intelligent classlessness. Edinburgh enticed the intelligentsia by the promise of joining Scotland's élite regardless of circumstances of birth. Leaders of the Enlightenment, therefore with a European audience, could range in social status

Edinburgh's beauty is no accident. The magnificent volcanic hills and large expanses of greenery may have been naturally endowed, but they have been fiercely defended by the citizens and its guardians. For many years the city was stigmatised with the well-deserved title of Auld Reekie when it was shrouded in thick acrid smoke, mainly produced from domestic coal-burning fires. The old City Corporation started, in 1960, its own green revolution which has since been sustained to culminate in the present high level of environmental awareness which means clean streets and clear unpolluted skies.

The first action was the introduction of "Smokeless Zones" within the city which banned the burning of smoke-producing fuels. These fuels not only produced large quantities of smoke but also sulphur dioxide, a major greenhouse gas. The Zones have been extended across the town and Edinburgh will be smokeless by 1995, the first city in Britain to achieve this.

The city's streets are main-tained to their high standard of cleanliness by a special squad system which targets heavily pedestrianised areas. The city has recycling facilities spread over the town and actively encourages people to save valuable resources such as paper, metal, plastic and rubber.

The main problem facing most European cities is the growth in car ownership. Edinburgh recognises this environmental problem and has addressed it by carrying out the most comprehensive nitrogen dioxide survey ever undertaken by any British city. This information is being used to plan ways of reducing the pollution, by having a city-wide cycle route provision and by far-reaching future planning which includes the building of a comprehensive metro system.

The need to protect our natural green areas, such as the Hermitage of Braid and Corstorphine Hill, have never been greater as land for development has become at a premium. The city has not shirked this responsibility and has introduced an Urban Nature Conservation Strategy which not from a minor laird (David Hume) to a wigmaker (Allan Ramsay), a poor rural schoolteacher (Thomas Ruddiman), and a penniless poet (Robert Fergusson).

Scotland's supreme cabinetmaker, Francis Brodie, who worked from the sign of Palladio's Head in the Lawnmarket, was a direct descendant of the Thanes of Brodie and had married into the Seafield family. His son, also Deacon of Wrights, inherited the aristocratic habit of maintaining two mistresses beyond his means. He turned to crime; and Deacon William Brodie, finally rumbled after a bungled raid on the Excise Office in Chessels Court, Canongate, was soon executed, carolling John Gray's ballad "Tis woman that ruins all mankind" as he went to the gallows. He was not only the inspirer of R. L. Stevenson's *Dr Jekyll and Mr Hyde,* but symbolised the split personality of the capital.

'Nothing can abolish the hills, unless it be a cataclysm of nature which shall subvert Edinburgh Castle itself and lay all her florid structures in the dust'

ROBERT LOUIS STEVENSON

only protects these 'Green Islands' but also ensures that green corridors exist between them to protect the bio-diversity of species. Visitor centres exist at the Hermitage of Braid where countryside rangers lead guided walks to further our knowledge of the wildlife which exists in these areas.

Although Edinburgh is still well supplied with wooded areas, much of its older stock has been decimated by Dutch Elm disease. To overcome this, plans are underway to introduce a new urban forest which will further enhance our wildlife.

To ensure the city is maintained to its present high standards and reacts to new environmental problems, both locally and globally, the District and Regional Councils consult with the public and then publish Environmental Action Plans which set targets for recycling, reducing pollution, protecting green areas and enhancing the environment. Edinburgh District Council was the first authority in Britain to publish Environmental Standards for its service delivery which promise to react to problems within set time limits.

In keeping with its standing as a Festival City, Edinburgh even has its own Festival of the Environment in May of each year. This brings together community groups, voluntary organisations, businesses and Government bodies in a week-long celebration of environmental issues. Over one hundred events take place from clean ups of the Water of Leith, which runs through the entire breadth of the city, to art events and educational ventures; there was even a sculpture at the top of the Mound last year made from recyclable material.

Edinburgh is rich in environmental beauty with rivers running through it, sea and beaches bordering it, large areas of woodland and is set amongst hills which have been left undeveloped. Its ancient buildings are protected to prevent change and present and future developments are based on environmental sustainability. The culture of environmentalism which exists will ensure that visitors in one hundred years time will see little change from what they see at present.

*'Arthur's Seat is
a high hill,
very rocky at
the top, and below
covered with
smooth turf,
on which sheep
were feeding'*

**DOROTHY
WORDSWORTH**

Physical dilapidation in the Old Town prompted that uniquely Enlightenment proposal in 1767 - a gridiron town on virgin land to the north, largely to a plan by the unknown James Craig. Conceived as an aristocratic suburb that would attract back to Scotland Scots aristocrats seduced by the comforts of London and abroad, it was to be thinly inhabited and that by persons of a certain rank. Professional people, and all classes below were to remain behind in the Old Town. No chance. The aristocrats remained in London. The first inhabitant of St Andrew's Square was David Hume, soon followed by the professions and the building of the Assembly Rooms. Princes Street was speedily transformed by commerce, and Queen Street occupied by the minor gentry, bankers and the law. The first New Town was followed by one downhill to the north, another encircling Calton Hill to the east, and one to the west. Walter Scott, who lived in Castle Street, observed sourly how the rivals of the northern New Town had brought thick yellow fog to the city. The aristocrats tried again: James Gillespie Graham designed a Baroque sequence of stupendous terraced houses, culminating in Moray Place, for the Earl of Moray. Although it had a higher cache than Queen Street with its dowry of dowagers, Edinburgh was inexorably becoming a city for the haut-bourgeois.

The New Towns changed Edinburgh for good. The pattern of recess during the four months of summer (when unemployed tramps were used to clear grass from between the cobbles of Charlotte Square with old scissors), the conviviality and the intellectual stimulus of the Old Town had vanished. The New Town stratified its population in separate and discreet locations: houses for the gentry (at George Street). Houses for the lesser gentry (Queen Street), houses for professional people, clerks and the like (Hill Street), houses for shopkeepers and the like (Rose Street). Similar patterns pertained in other New Towns. Cross streets - Castle, Frederick and Hanover - were not even houses, but tenements disguised to look like houses. The clubs of the Old Town died, and their social

function was replaced by late-evening suppers: but whereas the clubs had flourished in howffs and taverns, suppers were supped in house. Privacy entered Edinburgh's soul.

The Napoleonic Wars imprisoned that class of people accustomed to going on a Grand Tour throughout Europe within what they called the thin walls of England. Failing Europe, it was soon perceived that Edinburgh was the next best

A Georgian house, Charlotte Square

thing. Hugh Grecian Williams painted landscapes of Edinburgh demonstrating its similarity with Athens. And thus the classical split personality of Edinburgh - already apparent in the life of the city - was fossilised into stone: and the Old Town of Edinburgh was now seen as a savage memorial erupting through what was otherwise a serene and Attic landscape not unlike the Gulf of Corinth. In order to underscore the matter, Calton Hill was to become the Acropolis, and (by Jove!) they nearly made it. It was to the New Town, therefore, that the great schools, the art galleries and the government institutions came: in a magnificent Grecian architecture inspired by the Valhalla on Calton Hill from the hand of William Playfair, that truly justified Edinburgh's nickname.

The more the middle classes quit the Old Town for the New, the more the Old dissolved into a Hell: which, in turn, led to a further exodus which became a flood by the mid-century. Slum clearance in the Old Town, and the introduction of railways, led to tenements surging out into the countryside principally along the main roads to Leith, Dalry, Slateford, Morningside and Marchmont (many ancient villas that lay in their path were surrounded and ossified), interspersed with clusters of pioneering working-men's dwellings built by the Edinburgh Co-operative Building Company. The dominant characteristic of Victorian Edinburgh, as it basked in the glow of the achievements of Sir Walter Scott and his fellows, is one of marking time, save in the medical profession and in the Church. The established Church of Scotland ruptured in Edinburgh in 1843, leading to one and then another separate branch, so that by the 1890s, Edinburgh would be host to three General Assemblies of three different Kirks in the early summer time.

Physically, 19th-century Edinburgh pertains to the stone-walled suburb: detached mansions within their own walled gardens, gates automatically controlled from the house. Not even the frigid conversations that neighbours might have had

'Day by day, one new villa, one new object of offence, is added to another; the dismallest structures keep springing up like mushrooms'

ROBERT LOUIS STEVENSON

in Heriot Row would be had on the pavements outside these walled and elegant fortresses in Grange, Bruntsfield, Merchiston, Trinity, and later in Murrayfield, Colinton and Comiston. The countryside through which Dr Thomas Guthrie and his friends walked to meet Dr Thomas Chalmers to plan the Disruption, meeting Lord Cockburn walking from his villa back to town, became urban and suburban: and so enflamed Robert Louis Stevenson that he invited the burghers of Edinburgh to rise up and make the night hideous with arson.

Notions of class-consciousness, gentility and privacy, spawned by the New Town, became embedded in the Edinburgh suburban psyche. *"We want safe men here, you know, and so we generally get them"*, wrote the pioneering

LEEL AND THE ENVIRONMENT

The natural and built environment of the Lothians is one of Scotland's greatest assets and Edinburgh ranks among the finest cities in Europe. In 1991/92 Lothian & Edinburgh Enterprise Ltd invested £16 million in 250 projects to develop and protect this asset and to secure the future of inward investment for the region. The result has been significant improvements to the city, the towns and the rural areas of Lothian, including the creation of more than 125,000 sq ft of top-quality business space and the clearance of 137 hectares of derelict land for commercial use.

LEEL has initiated and progressed over 55 major property projects in 1991/92, attracting substantial investment from the private and public sectors.

Work has now begun on Scotland's biggest city-centre development of its type this century. The centre-piece of this £300 million project will be one of Europe's finest conference venues, the Edinburgh International Conference Centre. Equally important, however, will be the adjoining financial centre at the nine-acre site bounded by Lothian Road, the Western Approach Road and Morrison Street.

Few of LEEL's projects can be of more strategic or historical importance than the ten-acre site now being developed at Holyrood Road. Under the leadership of Sir Alick Rankin CBE, the Holyrood Brewery Foundation was established to mastermind this important project. The

town planner and reformer Sir Patrick Geddes scathingly about the gutlessness of the University. At the end of the century Edinburgh was caught up in the nationalist revival, with its flowering of music, publishing and art and the integration of the arts and crafts; philanthropy became rife. Geddes planned to re-inhabit the Old Town of Edinburgh as a university street like the High in Oxford. To that end, he was responsible not only for the construction of Ramsay Garden - wonderful flats for university lecturers - but for the rescue and restoration of many ancient fabrics in the Lawnmarket and the High Street for student lodgings and university buildings. Mosaicists, mural painters, artists, magazine designers, publishers and singers surged to help. Unfortunately, Geddes's enthusiasms were rapid: encountering obstacles, he left Scotland for Grenoble and then India, and the initiative foundered.

There Edinburgh might have rested but for the invention of the motor

Lorraine Murphy, Primary 5
Sighthill Primary School

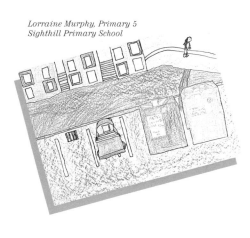

car. Between the Wars, those who were liberated by the purchase of their £90 Morris were able to drive out and buy a new bungalow: and the private, speculative house-builder began to cover acres of beautiful farmland with undifferentiated bungalows, associated shopping parades, the economical super cinema, and the smooth white roadhouse. Modernism, indeed, insulated Cramond and Easter Belmont. Surviving pockets of ancient high-density crumbling Edinburgh in the Old Town were cleared and rebuilt, and the powerless population exported to green-field peripheral estates, segregated from private-sector bungalows, with a lamentable absence of social foresight.

That, largely, is the explanation of Edinburgh as it remains today. After the Second World War, Edinburgh - like

project comprises two main parts: the £15 million Younger Universe, an exciting new visitor attraction, and a mixed development of quality housing, retail and commercial property.

LEEL is also involved in the removal of industrial dereliction on an enormous scale within the region. This will undoubtedly improve the environmental appeal of the area as a place to live in, and will help to secure future inward investment for Lothian. Indeed, thanks to a plan developed jointly with LEEL, Wayne Autcourt, a major subsidiary of the US conglomerate Dresser Industries, now has its UK head-quarters in Midlothian.

Much is being done in the city of Edinburgh too. Here, LEEL is investing £6 million to restore and develop the city's historic Old Town and in particular, its unique centre piece, the Royal Mile. To restore and preserve its character, LEEL has initiated a series of environmental renewal projects, incorporating the highest standards of quality, craftsmanship and attention to detail.

Edinburgh's skyline and architecture are among the most spectacular in Europe and much of it can now be admired after dark thanks to LEEL's 'Lighting Vision'.

Unique in its scale and design, this long-term project is illuminating landmark buildings and monuments throughout the city, and it is accelerating the project to get as much of the city completed as it can in time for the European Summit in December 1992.

LEEL are committed to working for the environment in Lothian Region. Much is being done. It is determined to see that the work continues enhancing the environment of Edinburgh and Lothian Region through 1992 and beyond.

every other major city in the western world - was periodically attracted and repelled by the necessity of matching rival cities in the production of modern office blocks, shopping centres, inner motorways and bypasses, perhaps blessed with fewer than elsewhere. The population of the Old Town slumped to almost nil in the mid 1960s, and it seemed as though the High Street would be turned into an office district. Enlightenment Edinburgh, for which Patrick Geddes in the 1890s, and again the Scottish Renaissance literati in the 1930s yearned, finally resurfaced, in the unlikely guise of an Arts Festival. It is to the Edinburgh Festival and Fringe, and to those glorious days when the pavements are packed at midnight and where illuminati from throughout the world jostle, that one now looks for signs of Edinburgh's daemon.

The population of the Old Town has risen threefold (to 7000) since

1970: although far short of a sustainable level, the trend is in the right direction. Shops have re-opened, hotels established, and major institutions are focused once more upon the *grande place*. There is better understanding now than there has been for perhaps 200 years as to the inherently European nature of the living patterns of old Edinburgh, the social value to the found in tenement form, the benefits of necessary action and inter-action between people.

Edinburgh's future as a successful European city will depend upon its ability to live up to the ambitions of the 4th-century Antioch orator Libianus: *"Well, it seems to me that the pleasantest, yes, and most profitable side of city life is*

EDINBURGH IN LOTHIAN: LOTHIAN IN EUROPE

Cllr Eric Milligan

Edinburgh is a beautiful city, but it is not just beautiful. Edinburgh contains the headquarters of some of Scotland's largest and most successful organisations, but it is not just a capital city. Edinburgh has been home to towering figures in the worlds of art, science, medicine and literature, but it is more than just a centre of excellence in human endeavour.

Edinburgh is more than just a city: it cannot be defined just by its buildings or its townscape.

To experience Edinburgh, you must use all your senses and faculties. As a short cut, for tourists in a hurry, intensive exposure to the poetry of McCaig and Garrioch is much more likely to convey a picture of the essential Edinburgh than the guided tours of the Old Town closes, and the classical but stark geometry of the New Town.

Perhaps better than anyone else, McCaig and Garrioch reflect an Edinburgh defined through its people and its non-physical qualities: through the chill of a clear November evening, the all-enveloping wrap of a haar drifting in from the Forth, the roar of the crowds behind the tenements of Tynecastle and Easter Road, or a

snatch of conversation overheard in a Cowgate bar or the Gairdens.

But what are the dimensions of this Edinburgh we are celebrating? What is Edinburgh's role and place in the world? Help in answering these questions is available close to us, having been articulated in Edinburgh a hundred years ago by one of the city's most famous residents. Sir Patrick Geddes, a biologist and town planner, came to be in Edinburgh and in 1902 saw the city functioning in the same way as a living organism would, being defined by dynamic living processes, and being functionally part of its surrounding environs.

For Geddes, Edinburgh was not, and could not be seen in stark isolation. Rather, Edinburgh and its surroundings represented for him a 'natural region', complete in terms of its physical, political, commercial and social aspects: "seldom is so full and dramatic set of contrasts crowded into one narrow region," he observed.

The geography and the wealth of Lothian's land and natural resources have combined to shape the economy of the region, and have produced a quality of life in this part of Scotland amongst the highest in Europe. From the eighteenth century *society and human intercourse; and that by Zeus is truly a city where these are most found - people in cities lose the habit of intimacy the further they live apart. The habit of friendship is matured by constant intercourse."*

The essence of civilised life, those habits of intimacy and intellectual exchange, could revive in Edinburgh - and make it a European role model for what we believe a city should be in the future. For it is a place that lives in the mind. As Robert Louis Stevenson wrote from Boulogne in 1872: *"After all, new countries, sun, music and all the rest can never take down our gusty, rainy, smoky, grim old city - the first place that it has been making for itself in the bottom of my soul - my heart is buried there - say, in Advocates Close!"*.

Robert Louis Stevenson

when Edinburgh was the centre of the European Enlightenment, Lothian in all its diversity of industry, agriculture, learning and culture has remained one of Europe's great regions.

Geddes' ideas have helped shape the way that we look at the world and its social organisation. A hundred years ago, Geddes saw Europe's future as an ecology of interconnecting city-regions. Significantly, 'the Europe of the Regions' is being promoted again, this time within the context of the European Community, and with such vigour as to cause some national governments to ponder uneasily about their own future role and functions.

The relevance and perception of his vision has not dimmed over time. If anything, the complex connections between Edinburgh, its region, Scotland and Europe bind even tighter. New dynamics exist and have been created in this latter part of the twentieth century, and the role of Edinburgh and its region will be a critical and essential part of the new Europe. The legacy of our past links with Europe are all around us, in our architecture, in street names, our

legal system and other institutions. For us, as guardians and observers in the new-age development, it is a privilege to witness the rebirth and reassertion of our region's links with Europe.

In preparing for the future, we need to recreate a positive vision of Lothian in Europe and Europe in Lothian, to make our children and people truly European citizens.

A hundred years ago, the Geddes Outlook Tower was built at the top of the High Street. Through this tower, and its Camera Obscura periscope, Geddes sought to demonstrate the fundamental interdependence of the city and its region, and the links to the world beyond.

The message for us is clear. There is no future for Edinburgh, Scotland and Europe in a retreat behind the city walls. Our land cannot be divided up into small urban and rural parcels, to be administered introspectively, backs turned against the world beyond. The theme for the future has already been given to us in the Outlook Tower. From city, region, Europe, and globally in ever widening spatial circles, Edinburgh and Lothian are intricately bound into the ecology of a wider community.

'The winds, instead of rushing down with impetuosity, whirl about in eddies, and become still more dreadful. On these occasions it is almost impossible to stir out of doors'

EDWARD TOPHAM

*'If I were to
choose a spot
from which
the rising sun
could be seen
to the greatest
possible advantage,
it would be
called Salisbury'*

SIR WALTER SCOTT

Edinburgh from Salisbury Crags. *W. B. Scott (City Art Centre, Edinburgh)*

AN EDINBURGH DAY

ALAN TAYLOR

Alan Taylor is the Features and Literary Editor
of *Scotland on Sunday*.
In another life he was a librarian, in which capacity
he edited the *Assistant Librarian* and served
on the Management Committee of the Booker Prize.
As a freelance writer he contributed to
diverse newspapers, magazines and books.
He appears irregularly on radio and television
and is currently trying unsuccessfully
to keep happy several publishers.

*'...I was bushed
and ready
for bed,
well-spent
in well-set
Edinburgh'*

The train from London slips into Waverley Station around six in the morning while, in Auden's words, "well-set Edinburgh" sleeps. Arriving under cover of darkness, you take the city by surprise. But you too are surprised. Expecting a somnambulant city, the noise in the station is like an assault in a monastery. Train doors close with the clang of a vault, the cries and whispers of passengers and railway staff are amplified as in an echo chamber. Killing time before disembarking, you are in that happy limbo situated between departure and arrival, when you know that you are going somewhere but are not exactly sure of your destination.

Almost thirty years ago the writer Neil McCallum described Waverley as the "largest, dirtiest and gloomiest station in Britain". That was not true then, and it is even less true now. At this hour of the morning machines emitting a low whine buff the marble on the station concourse, sprucing it up for the day ahead. At six the newsagent's kiosk opens and then come commuters, drawn as if by magnets, bustling to catch the half-hourly trains for Glasgow. There is something sinful about watching people scurrying to work.

In no time at all, the station is transformed. Lowry-like men and women pour down the wind-whipped steps from Princes Street or tumble down the hill from the Waverley Bridge, running not necessarily because they are late but because the gradient is so steep. It is the first hint that Edinburgh is more rock bun than pancake.

After nine, the human traffic in the station thins out. The only way out of the station is up. Emerging on to Waverley Bridge, the city's landmarks vie for attention. In other cities, you are always keen to put some distance between yourself and the railway station. But arriving at Waverley, you land in the heart of Edinburgh; no play has a more dramatic opening. To the north is the Scott Monument, a sooty rocket built as a memorial to Sir Walter Scott, the *soi-disant* "Wizard of the North". Peering to the west is the Castle, glowering or towering over the city depending on your mood. To the east is the rococo Balmoral Hotel, while southward lies the Old Town with its myriad closes and imposing tenements.

'...the scent was so offensive, that we were forced to hold our noses as we passed the streets, and take care where we trod for fear of disobliging our shoes'

JOSEPH TAYLOR

Hislop, smith and farrier. *The Cavaye Collection of Thomas Begbie Prints (City Art Centre, Edinburgh)*

It is time to make a decision. Parked in the rank, taxi drivers are immersed in the *Daily Record.* Across the street is an open-decked tour bus promising the sights of the city "and environs" in just two hours. On its top deck four Japanese tourists offer passable impressions of blocks of ice. "Chilly for September," mutters a guide with well-rehearsed understatement. A piper draws his pipes from his bag into which he throws a few coins to inspire passers-by. On the corner of Princes Street the postcard seller ('English Spoken, American Understood') recommends taking the "weight of your feet" in the Hebrides in Market Street, or the "He-brides" as it was once called in a gay guide to the city.

It is early doors, as they say around here, for a beer or a nip of whisky, but around ten the bar is host to a handful of shift workers from the railway, the post office on the North Bridge and the *Scotsman* newspaper. In the dim light a television flickers but no one pays it much attention. Breakfast is a cup of coffee and some desultory chatter on the state of Scottish football. "Some goal the boy Durrant scored for the 'Gers on Saturday," says one, shaking his toothless head in wonderment. No one agrees or disagrees but the landlord's eyebrows go up like a first-night curtain. Somehow you just know he is not a Rangers' supporter.

Outside the wind has dropped but there is a fine drizzle in the air. Edinburgh, as Robert Louis Stevenson wrote, pays cruelly for her *"high seat in one of the vilest climates under the heaven".* The sickly, tubercular writer had more reason than most to rue the weather of the town where he was brought up but no one who lives here for any time, not even the purple prose writers of the tourist board, can be oblivious to the elements. Edinburgh, added Stevenson, *"is liable to be drenched with rain, to be buried in cold sea fogs out of the east, and powdered with snow as it comes southward from the Highland hills".* Though it may no longer be true to say, as it undoubtedly was in Stevenson's day, that the delicate die early in Edinburgh, its climate has inevitably imposed itself on the character of the people.

'When God Himself takes to panorama-painting, it turns out strangely beautiful'

FELIX MENDELSSOHN

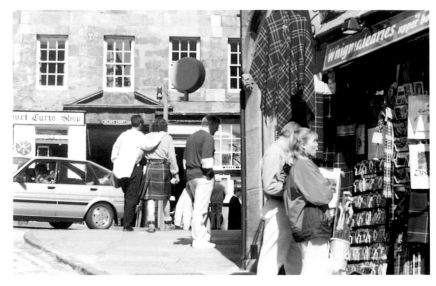

'The Scots
dialect is
singularly rich
in terms of reproach
against the winter
wind. Snell, blae, nirly
and scowthering are
all words that
carry a shiver
with them'

**ROBERT LOUIS
STEVENSON**

Sunny days of azure skies, as the poet Alastair Reid acknowledged, are as likely as not to be greeted not with joyous appreciation but with the three crone's chorus: "*We'll pay for it! We'll pay for it! We'll pay for it!*" Hardened citizens cope with meteorological vicissitudes with an expectation of the worst. Thus, no matter what the time of year, Edinburghers dress for "all weathers".

Collar-up, I turn right then head up Fleshmarket Close and into the Old Town which, until the 18th century and the building of the New Town, *was* Edinburgh. The High Street, falling for a mile from the Castle to Holyrood House, looks from the air like the bones of a fish. At street level it is infinitely interesting, where tourists rigged out in tartan mingle with hoary locals hanging around the betting shops or the newspaper stand opposite what was once the Tron church.

At Di Placido, the deli opposite John Knox's House, Ernie gives gratis a seminar on contemporary cinema. Not many doors down, the ubiquitous Dr Johnson stayed with James Boswell. At Boyd's Inn (happily no longer extant), Johnson asked to have his lemonade made sweeter. With his greasy fingers a Basil Fawlty among waiters took a lump of sugar and plonked it in the lemonade. Johnson promptly threw it out the window. When the pair emerged to go to Boswell's house, the night was dusky and odiferous despite the city magistrates clamping down on people flinging rubbish on to the street. "I can smell you in the dark!" Johnson told a worried Boswell. Two hundred and more years later the High Street, or the Royal Mile as it is commonly known, has succumbed to gentrification but it still exerts charm. From here you can go any which way but there's a good coffee house tucked in behind St Giles Cathedral. About eleven is the ideal time to eavesdrop on lawyers from the nearby High Court discussing cases or, more likely, the weekend ahead.

At the crossroads between the High Street and George IV Bridge, where at the height of the Scottish Enlightenment it was said you could meet any number of geniuses, you have various options. You could either head down the Mound towards Princes Street and be swallowed up by the lunchtime shoppers, hike to the Castle and indulge in some serious sightseeing, or turn into George IV Bridge dropping down into the Grassmarket via bijou Victoria Street to catch whatever entertainment is on offer. There is a down-and-out singing Sinatra in the middle of the Grassmarket, belting out *My Way* with admirable, if tuneless, defiance. A bevy of brewing students from Heriot-Watt University applaud. "What about Dean Martin's *Little Old Wine Drinker?*" shouts one, and the drunk crooner duly obliges, brandishing his lager can as if it were a microphone. Not so long ago the Grassmarket was one of the most unsavoury parts of central Edinburgh but in recent years it has also been gentrified. The dank unsavoury bars have been modernised, and chic clothes shops, antique emporia and Italian restaurants conspire to create a continental atmosphere. In bygone days the Grassmarket was a point of departure in more senses than one. From the White Hart Inn horse-drawn coaches left for London but it was also in the Grassmarket that many unfortunates were executed in public. Edinburgh was a dangerous and violent place and in 1736 there occurred an infamous riot, when the mob lynched Captain Porteous. Porteous had been sentenced to death after ordering his Guard to fire on the crowd when they rioted after an unpopular execution. Several people were wounded and one man was killed. However, to public dismay, Porteous was subsequently reprieved and the mobs response was to storm the Tolbooth prison to drag him to his doom. Needless to say such behaviour is frowned on in Edinburgh today, which is the soul of propriety, at least on the surface. But beneath the veneer of respectability, generations of commentators have detected another city, with a dark and sinister air about it, the literary exemplar of which is Stevenson's *Dr Jekyll and Mr Hyde*. The idea of the Double pervades the literature of the city though one

'Dr Johnson acknowledged that the breadth of the street, and the loftiness of the buildings on each side, made a noble appearance'

JAMES BOSWELL

Porteous mob. *Artist unknown (City Art Centre, Edinburgh)*

*'...and so,
to escape from
a vulgar London
association of ideas,
it was named
Princes Street,
after the future
Duke of York'*

JAMES GRANT

feels it does not exist so much in fact as in fiction. Still it is a game to play in your mind while you tour around. Could that starched lawyer possibly be an embezzler? What's that minister doing dropping into a bar in the middle of the afternoon? Wasn't that a well-known newspaper editor at the door of a massage parlour?

As the day wears on and the light changes so too does the city. Edinburgh is really a series of villages and the character alters as you move between them. Portobello, Leith, Newhaven, Cramond and South Queensferry form an arc round the Firth of Forth but each has its own ambience; seaside resort, working port, fishing village, stockbroker suburb, dormitory town. They are at once distinct yet quintessentially Edinburgh. But it is in the centre of town where the inhabitants mingle. At five o'clock in the Central Library on George IV Bridge many of the desks in the reference section are taken, mainly by uniformed school children or ancient autodidacts who flit from Keesing's to Amateur Gardening, the

collected works of Marx and Engels to Black's Medical Dictionary. Rarely these days will you find a tramp drying his socks on the library's radiators but there is still a feeling of security about the place, a home from home for those who don't have one.

Edinburgh, said a former Lord Provost, was a city of three Bs: *beer, biscuits* and *books*, the first two in acknowledgement of local industries, the last because Edinburgh was not only a city with a venerable university but also at the hub of British and world publishing. But even in the library, books must compete with the bleep of the computer and the clank of the photocopier; it is no longer a sepulchral place of study. For that you must either cross the road to the National Library or head along George IV Bridge and into Greyfriars' churchyard. It is too

AN EMBARRASSMENT OF GIFTS

The Rt. Hon. Norman Irons

As a city with many international links, Edinburgh sends her Lord Provost and other emissaries abroad, and regularly receives goodwill ambassadors in return. It is customary on such occasions to exchange gifts – usually something artistic and typical of the giver's home base.The only snag to these universal expressions of goodwill is that eventually there comes a moment when the cupboards in the City Chambers will hold no more.

Edinburgh is given about 100 gifts a year. When a gift is first received it is placed on public display in the City Chambers. Then, after a time, these more recent gifts must be moved out of the display case to make way for a fresh batch. It would be difficult to keep every gift belonging to the city on public view and yet ensure their security. So the great majority must go into store .

What lies behind the double-locked door? Bronze medallions, graciously accepted by Lord Provosts now long departed, nestle alongside decorated plates and inscribed crockery. Flags, of all sizes, abound. There are clocks, vases, pictures, examples of marquetry, many illustrated books, and a very realistic model of a British Army tank from Germany.

The most eye-catching item in the room is a fearsome knobkerry – a wooden club with a round head with spikes in it. This gift was given to former Lord Provost Eleanor McLaughlin during an official visit to Edinburgh's twin city of Kiev in 1990. The knobkerry looks so unfriendly that it is obviously a Ukrainian witticism. Whether the convener of Kiev City Council actually uses this type of gavel seems unlikely; for one thing it would ruin the table.

Here is a genuine gavel. It is inscribed, "Made by Ian Kirk, Tynecastle Secondary School. Presented to the Edinburgh Corporation, March 1954". Ian, where are you now?

There is at least one samovar in the collection. It seems a pity that it should be gathering dust here, in the midst of a tea-drinking nation.

Among the boxes there are a surprising number of pieces of Chinese art, considering that Xi'an is relatively recent as twinning links go. Over there is a fine bronze head of a greyhound, a memento from a Powderhall occasion. In another corner, looking just a wee bit out of place in otherwise serious company, is a cheerful barrel of Crabbie's Green Ginger Wine.

Perhaps the most solemn item in the collection is that commemorating a wartime tragedy which was felt particularly keenly in the city – the loss of the cruiser, *HMS Edinburgh* on a hazardous voyage to Russia in 1942. The exhibit, which was presented by an association of survivors and shipmates, is a roll of honour, containing the names of 59 members of the ship's company who went down with *HMS Edinburgh*.

These gifts all speak of important days to those who gave them, and the Lord Provost who received them. The story of Edinburgh as an international city could be written just from the store room of gifts.

cold to linger long in the latter, though, and soon one resorts to the bosomy warmth of Sandy Bell's, a pub in Forrest Road. It is a disappointing day because Hamish Henderson, poet, singer and doyen of the School of Scottish Studies, is not, as Robert Burns wrote of Tam O' Shanter, "boozin' at the nappy".

There is, however, a fiddler tuning up, a glass of beer in front of me and a Scotch pie in the microwave. If we are what we eat, I hesitate to say too much about the phenomenon of the pie, which is a fundamental part of the Scottish cuisine. It is said that the grease from these pies oiled the wheels of just about everything from milk carts to Sherman tanks, not to mention commerce and fortune. Somebody somewhere must have made his fortune out of pies but to Scots the

The arrival of the mail coach at The Black Bull. *William Turner (City Art Centre, Edinburgh)*

quality of a pie is inextricably connected to its cheapness and its ability to satisfy the appetite. Made of a cardboard crust filled with minced meat of indeterminate origin, the pie is gastronomically tasty but a nutritionist's nightmare. The one in Sandy Bell's evokes the great pies of the past; it is a Proust's *petite madeleine* among pies.

As night falls, the streets go quiet. It is too late now to cross the Meadows and take in Bruntsfield, Marchmont and Morningside, the famous suburb where it used to be said the well-to-do watch the world through net curtains. Instead I head off down Lauriston Road, past the Infirmary and the fire station and towards Tollcross and the tenement where the poet Norman MacCaig lives. MacCaig, now in his ninth decade, has lived in Edinburgh all his life, despite his own admission to being "three-quarters" Gael. He was born in the heart of the New Town, in Dundas Street, surrounded on all sides by the classical architecture of Georgian Edinburgh, a fitting beginning for a man whose poetry is imbued with classic lines. He went to the Royal High School and then to Edinburgh University where he read classics. He made a career as a teacher, ending up as headmaster at

'...six, seven, eight storeys high were the houses; storey piled above storey, as children build with cards'

CHARLES DICKENS

'The old
town, seen
as we saw it,
in the obscurity of
a rainy day, hardly
resembles the work
of men; it is more
like a piling up
of rocks'

**DOROTHY
WORDSORTH**

Parson's Green primary school on the east side of the city. When he married, he and his wife Isabel moved to a handsome redbrick tenement in Leamington Terrace in Tollcross.

For many it is a place of pilgrimage. MacCaig's migrations around the city make him pre-eminently its Poet Laureate. He has been everywhere, seen it all, tried to define it, say something about the people who live in it. Even to people who do not read poetry his cracked voice, twinkling eyes, acid wit and smirking sense of humour embody the spirit of the city. We go to the Abbotsford in Rose Street, his old haunt, where in the orange light the characters change by the hour. At opening time it is habituated by nine-to-fivers, civil servants and insurance men fortifying themselves for the trek home. An hour later smart shop assistants from Jenner's

'There is no street in Europe more spectacular than Princes Street; it is absolutely operatic'

HENRY JAMES

department store descend. There is a lull from six to seven, in what is wryly called "the happy hour", when *"the connoisseurs of the morose"*, as Hugh MacDiarmid, MacCaig's late sparring partner, described them, hog the bar. Then after eight come the social drinkers, finding relief in conversation in a pub without a television, juke-box or fruit machines. MacCaig, cigarette in one hand, glass of Macallan in the other, is still the ringmaster. Later, hanging around for a late bus outside Waverley Station, I think of his poem, 'London to Edinburgh', the last one in his *Collected Poems*.

"I'm waiting for the moment when the train crosses the Border
and home creeps closer
at seventy miles an hour."
At closing time Norman said, "Come back to the house."
"But I was bushed and ready for bed, well-spent in well-set Edinburgh."

The Horse Fair in the Grassmarket. *James Howe (City Art Centre, Edinburgh)*

THE ESTABLISHMENT CITY

SIR NICHOLAS FAIRBAIRN

Sir Nicholas Fairbairn QC is one of the most
colourful characters in Scottish politics.
A Member of Parliament since 1974,
Sir Nicholas confounded many pundits by
again holding his Perth and Kinross seat in April 1992.
Describing himself as a journalist, painter, writer, lawyer
and politician, he was Solicitor General
for Scotland from 1979-82 and has been a member
of the Edinburgh Festival Council since 1971.

*'...the great creative,
roistering spirit which
created the city,
after God laid the
foundations in rock,
might re-emerge.'*

Black is the denial of light and it absorbs heat and warmth. White rejects light. If you doubt me, put your hand on a taxi and a caravan in the sun.

Let me first indulge in the experiences of darkness and the psychology of blackness. All of us spend nine months in the dark after our conception in the black before we are thrust painfully into the light for such time as we are permitted, until we are recommitted to eternal darkness and the unknown. Yes unknown, for that is what darkness creates. In the dark we fear noises, attacks, or the devils and ghosts, which in the light we cannot see and do not fear.

Edinburgh wears black, and beneath its soucience there is a lot of heat, but it is hidden and contained. It is a city of confused identity and thus reluctant to express itself. Like the middle classes it has the dual difficulties of fearing inferiorty, and practising superiority. Unlike Glasgow, where each is his own person, the citizens of Edinburgh are acutely and nervously self-conscious of who they are, or worse still, who they are not. It is black in its profile and grey in its population.

And although Edinburgh is probably the most beautiful sculpture God and man came together to create it has had more periods of dark and light than almost any other city. Prior to the departure of the Stuart Kings to rule England,

South View of Canongate Kirk, *Parr after Elphinstone. (City Art Centre, Edinburgh)*

Edinburgh was a mighty dour town - mean, cross and dirty. Gardy loo (watch it, or get a load of shit on your head) was practically the national anthem. That was a really black time, in which every resentment was adjured, and it culminated in the enthronement of Calvinism under the aegis of John Knox, who having caught syphilis in Geneva, from one of his many whores, introduced misogyny as another part of his doctrine of hatred and doctrinal deprivation. That masochistic time lasted for another century, which is shown by the bleak, mean tenements of the Old Town, until, wondrously, the Union of the Parliaments occurred in 1707; from which time, Scotland prospered, and became the most civilised part of Europe and Edinburgh had amongst us the Bourbon Kings of France in exile, the most enlightened philosophers and thinkers and visitors from all European civilisation.

In the eighteenth and nineteenth century the dark of Edinburgh was turned to incandescent light by the works of Hume, Adam, Playfair, Scott, Raeburn, Ramsay, and a thousand others, but black kept creeping back in. Auguste Edourt, the great French silhouettist, found Edinburgh the breeding ground for his glorious black portrait, which illustrates the cosmopolitan and racy composition of those who dwelt here and those who came here. The only exception to our enlightenment was the Kirk, which remained like a black cloud, doom laden and threatening. Guilt in the fear of sin is the fierce progenitor of threat.

The threatening Kirk splintered into multiple threatening judges of men, while the judges remained jolly and enlightened; and when decanters of port were banned by some puritan freak from their benches, they put it in their inkwells instead and sucked their quills. In our generation the Kirk has become the Department of Sociology - earthly not divine and the bench has become the department of self-righteousness, the progenitor of the classless and meaningless society, treacherous to the inheritance of the swash-buckling excellence of those who proceeded them. But then I suppose that is political properness at its worst. The Minister and Presbytery of St. Giles, Knox's Cathedral, have replaced the great Victorian West window which adulated and illustrated the life of our Lord and Saviour Jesus Christ and his Disciples, with a window dedicated to Robert Burns, the greatest fornicator and drunk of his time. I do not object to his habits, I merely object to the Kirk's sociological hypocrisy.

Victorians unconsciously invented the middle class by creating the professions - before which time there was no substantial wedge between landowners and wage earners. Thus the great Georgian New Town of Edinburgh was not conceived by town planners, it was designed by enthusiastic amateurs. Ann Raeburn, the great portrait painter's wife, designed Ann Street. An army captain designed St Andrew's Church in George Street. Nobody designed the Castle. But when the professions arrived, each with their set of proprieties and rules and self-respect and puff, the creative spirit of the imaginative amateur was suffocated under a sludge of professional porridge and the dead hand of self-righteousness imbued its character. It was institutionalised, deep frozen. It became a hive of the half high, half haughty. The buzz went out of the bees and the bees just let 'bs' take over.

'Edinburgh
is a city of churches,
as though it
were a place of
pilgrimage'

**ROBERT LOUIS
STEVENSON**

There was, it is true, a Victorian exultation of Edinburgh (perhaps unfortunate since the hubris of another perfect town like Dublin was spoilt by the Victorians) but more recent 'improvers' have cast greyness back on the city: Basil Spence, Robert Matthew, Johnston-Marshall and Reiach. They have made grey and dark and tedious and dull, the glory of that Edinburgh, which for a great century was the beacon of Europe. They who were in charge, as listers of their protection, eradicated four great buildings, The New Club, Scottish Widows glorious palace and the magnificent Life Association Buildings, not to mention George Square. "Lighten our darkness we beseech thee O Lord."

Unquestionably contemporary Edinburgh is a thrawn place - its gatherings are parochial and self-righteous as all establishments tend to be. Those who attend their functions, as they call them, think it is grand to attend, and those

EDINBURGH – THE CAPITAL OF INGENUITY

Charles Winter

In the darkest winter days of late 1785, when the French were thinking of getting rid of their king and neither the Germans nor the Italians were a single nation, leading Edinburgh businessmen met in one of the aisles of the High Kirk of St Giles. Their designs were of Mammon rather than of God and the result of their meeting was the establishment of the Edinburgh Chamber of Commerce and Manufacturers.

Ingenuity – the solution of problems – has been and still is the characteristic of both Edinburgh and the country of which it is the capital and the early acts of the Chamber underlined this point. Having improved the lighthouse on May Island at the entrance of the Firth of Forth, the Chamber devoted its attention to that hardy annual of businessmen, tardy postal services. At the instigation of the Chamber and for the first time in the world, mail was date-stamped.

An equal concern for time was shown in 1861 when a deputation arranged for the firing of the daily one o'clock gun, a practice of interest to tourists and of help to citizens even today.

There is barely an activity in Edinburgh business life where that desire to improve a practice, make more efficient a product or simplify a procedure is not a long-running but still meaningful element.

In my life outside the Chamber of Commerce, I am vice-chairman of The Royal Bank of Scotland. A couple of centuries ago, my opposite number in our rival bank in the city had enough time to design the world's first steamship and also produce a warship for the King of Sweden. In keeping with his practical bent, his reward from the monarch was half a dozen seeds for a newly developed vegetable which to this day is still known as a Swede.

Bankers have far too busy lives these days for such dramatic diversification but we still represent an industry vital to the health of Edinburgh, with our own tradition of practical banking innovation. My own bank can for example boast among its "inventions" the overdraft, coloured bank notes, bank branches and mobile banks, whilst we and our Edinburgh competitors can, in these high tech days, point to trail-blazing roles in

they attend upon think they are even grander. Blessed are the humble for they shall inherit middle class values. There are constellations of little planetary cliques - the university with its otiose staff club, the financial institutions - secret, grey and incestuous, the lawyers, the accountants, the galleries, the Kirk, host to the annual hypocrisy of the General Assembly of the Church of Scotland obsessed with "The Gospel, Worship and Caring", but little mention of everlasting life and more concerned with the sins of South Africa than the sins of Scotland, of which the greatest in Edinburgh is the lack of fun or a sense of fun.

It is difficult to see (in the age of the classless society, which means a society of meaningless people with no style, no grit, no difference, and therefore, no significance) how Edinburgh can relieve itself of the grey pallor of its nature, or its present nature. But let us take heart. Glasgow is a grim city and its citizens were

John Knox

home banking and international payment systems.

We are only part of the financial services industry, dominated by life insurance offices, investment trusts and specialist advisers, which gives the city its distinctive business profile.

It is that practical approach to matters that is the hallmark of Edinburgh and its business community. Even the professions, often seen elsewhere as introverted and detached from reality, are in this city firmly rooted in reality. The lawyers, the doctors, the civil servants, the accountants and the bankers are widely seen, by themselves and as well as by their colleagues and competitors to the south and further afield, as more closely in touch with the needs of their customers.

Edinburgh is not of course just a city of the professions, although it does have a greater proportion of people so employed than most cities of its size. It is a significant city of trade and manufacture. Many of the great traditional industries have atrophied, but others have come forward to take their place. We can

no longer claim to be the centre of the world publishing and printing technology, although there are still a number of companies carrying on that tradition. Our long-standing reputation in brewing is in safe hands and a number of new technology based industries ply their trade within the city.

Of course, being the capital forming the jagged northern edge of an offshore island to Europe, the city is long used to having to combat the drag of centralisation. It is no coincidence that most of the weapons to fight that pull - the telephone, television, fax machines and even the humble postage stamp - were all invented by Scots. It is a question of that ingenuity again.

We are confident that the business community of Edinburgh will relish the opportunities offered by the new Europe and will be true to its reputation in being practical enough to combat any challenges or disadvantages. We are looking forward to rejoining - and I emphasise that word - the European business sphere which for most of our history has been the focus of our trade.

glout folk until twenty years ago. Now it shines and they sparkle. Who would have thought it possible?

So the same could happen to Edinburgh and the great creative, roistering spirit which created the city, after God laid the foundations in rock, might re-emerge. And the dull, drilled, docile masses of the professionals might lose their deadly hand and their deadly dull one too. Those amputations might lift the pall from one of the most fascinating cities on this earth. Pray God it will. The motto of the city is *"Nisi Dominus Frustra"* (If God doesn't want it to happen it won't!). I trust He wants it to happen.

GLIMPSING THE ESTABLISHMENT

Any weekday morning on the Mound, if you choose your moment, you will observe a succession of solitary and soberly dressed gentlemen walking at leisurely pace uphill towards the High Street. Their dress is almost a uniform: pinstripe suit, homburg, walking stick or rolled umbrella. It sets them apart from the throng but only just.

Unnoticed by virtually every passer-by, many of these dignified pedestrians are the judges of Scotland's supreme court; the others are Queen's Counsel or junior advocates. All are making their way from their homes in the Georgian New Town to the law courts in Parliament Square. In the afternoon they will retrace their steps, released from the soporific atmosphere of the courtroom, their spirits uplifted by the incomparable view of the valley of Princes Street at dusk, and the Forth beyond.

This vignette, which is one of the small traditions of Edinburgh, is made possible by two things. The first is the compact nature of Scotland's capital city, which permits these distinguished men to live graciously within walking distance of their work; the second says something about the essentially egalitarian nature of Scottish society.

The informal procession up the Mound is one of the few occasions on which that nebulous entity, the Edinburgh establishment, may be actually sighted and positively identified. The Law, which may be fairly described as the very bedrock of any claim by Edinburgh to leadership, is undoubtedly one essential component of that establishment.

To obtain an impressive glimpse of Edinburgh's servants of the Law at their work-place, enter Parliament House at any reasonable hour and stroll casually into the spacious elegance of Parliament Hall. There you are virtually certain to see a fair number of gowned and wigged advocates, accompanied by their instructing solicitors, pacing back and forth in earnest discussion. Traditionally the higher echelons of the law were very much a male preserve, but nowadays the membership of the bar includes many women.

The second great pillar of the Edinburgh establishment is the Church. It is true that the Kirk no longer has the pervasive influence that it exercised over the lives of former generations. Yet the General Assembly, held annually on the Mound in May, is still a notable event in the Edinburgh calendar. For some ten days ministers and elders, having

Tanfield, the meeting place of the General Assembly of the Free Church of Scotland. *W. Forrest after W. Bonnar*

been commissioned to do so by every presbytery in Scotland, congregate in the capital. In the sombre precincts of the Assembly Hall they conduct the business of the Church, which means in effect that they debate all the great issues affecting Scottish life. It has been said with some truth that the General Assembly of the Church of Scotland is the closest thing Scotland has to her old Parliament.

For 400 years at least, ordinary Scots demonstrated a great respect for learning, for scholars and for the advantages of an education. This worthy tradition, which has not yet died out, inspired innumerable benefits not only to Scotland but indirectly to the world at large. In Edinburgh the great powerhouse in this regard proved to be the University of Edinburgh, founded in 1582 by Edinburgh Town Council. Over the centuries, the distinguished record of this ancient seat of learning earned it a place in the city's establishment that it has never lost.

What about the Scottish aristocracy, the ancient noble families? Where are they to be found in the Edinburgh establishment? Their role is certainly not a prominent one. They are shy creatures, scarce on the ground, not instantly recognisable to the man in the street. They may provide the occasional politician, but he (or she) is rather more likely to be encountered at the top table during the annual general meeting of some charitable institution. The chances will be that the noble patron lives furth of Edinburgh.

What are some of the other elements that comprise the Edinburgh establishment? The higher branches of the bureaucratic tree that grows within St Andrew's House undoubtedly provide many worthy members; while in a capitalist society, bankers and indeed anyone involved in Edinburgh's burgeoning financial services sector must also qualify.

One suspects that Edinburgh's club life, once renowned, is no longer the social force it once was; you no longer must be a member, but all those who are, are probably in the Establishment as well. Membership of a golf club with a famous name may well be a more reliable indicator today!

It used to be said that Edinburgh was not a place, but a state of mind. It's still true. What's more, Edinburgh regards it as a compliment!

'You go to dinner, the East wind is blowing chillily from hostess to host. You go to church, a bitter East wind is blowing in the sermon'

ALEXANDER SMITH

*'City
of mist
and rain and
blown grey
places'*

ALFRED NOYES

The Rev. Robert Walker skating on Duddingston Loch, *Sir Henry Raeburn (National Gallery of Scotland)*

FROM THE WEST

SUSAN DALGETY

The photographs in
this section are from
a project involving

all sectors of the
community in Wester
Hailes working in
groups to produce
music, photographs,
prose and poetry.

Susan Dalgety has been
editor of the *Wester Hailes Sentinel* since 1986
and before that was a full-time mother and part-time
shelf stacker at Prestos.
She has lived in Wester Hailes for ten years
and was elected the Labour District Councillor
for the Shandon ward in the area in May 1992.

A DAY
IN THE
LIFE

"If you take my laddies to Wester Hailes, I'll sue for custody and win." With this empty threat from my estranged husband ringing in my ears, my two young sons and I left our comfortable, but broken, suburban home and embarked on our biggest adventure to date – we moved into Wester Hailes. And ten years later we're happily still here.

As I suspected, my husband did not sue for custody but in 1988 a woman, living only a few stairs away from us, lost the custody battle for her five-year-old son – simply because she lived in one of Edinburgh's peripheral housing estates.

A DAY IN THE LIFE

A judge, no doubt one of Edinburgh's great and good, decided in his legal wisdom, that the young boy would have a better upbringing if he was to live with his father in the Shetland Isles. He accepted that the mother was a caring, capable woman. That the boy did not want to be separated from his mum, his school and his friends – but all to no avail. The judge decreed that Wester Hailes was not a fit place to bring up a young child – and so a mother lost her son because of her address.

So what kind of place is this Wester Hailes? This estate that fills a member of the Scottish legal system with such horror and alarm?

Quite simply, it is a large, public sector housing estate, nestling under the dour splendour of the Pentland Hills, with a population of 12,000 working-class folk who share the same hopes, dreams and problems of working-class communities anywhere in Europe.

Built in the late sixties and early seventies, it stands as one of the last monuments to the failure of British town planning and housing policies of the late sixties.

It was constructed near the end of the high-rise mania that gripped the architectural community at that time and nearly 40% of the homes were those ill-conceived "streets in the sky". The rest were modern tenements, whose design was based loosely on the Old Town tenements which so delight Edinburgh's tourists. But that was where the resemblance to traditional Edinburgh was to end.

A wave of cost-cutting exercises meant that the original plans for a high street with shops, pubs and cafés were abandoned. There was no secondary school, no library, no health centre, no police station. The children had no playgrounds. There were no youth clubs – or jobs – for the teenagers. There was no local industry and the residents had to struggle with a hopelessly inadequate public transport system to get to work and play. But there were car parking spaces in abundance.

'You're a lesser class of person if you're frae Wester Hailes. People say that's not true, ken, lawyers and that, but it is true. The minute you say Wester Hailes, ken, you see a wee reaction from them. I've noticed it when I've been in tae interviews and I've got experience of work. It's discrimnation just because of the area you're living in'

'Like I got told wi the crisis loans that it's only 40% of the people that apply that actually get it. You've got to be either dying or you've got to be in some real difficulties, ken I mean difficulties! Like you could be sitting wi nae electricity and nae food for a fortnight and that's no a crisis'

Training opportunities with Wester Hailes Management Agency see page 5

SPECIAL EDITION

WESTER HAILES SENTINEL

THE HEART OF THE COMMUNITY

Platform ADULT LEARNING CENTRE UPDATE see Page 2 96 WESTER HAILES ROAD EDINBURGH EH14 2SW TEL: 031 458 5082

WELCOME TO YOUR DREAM HOME

WINNERS - Lianne Harrison (left) and Brian Whitelaw took the honours in the 1991 Fun Run.

The McWhirter family entertain their VIP guests in their new Hailesland home

WE'RE OFF AND RUNNING

THERE is still eight months to go, but preparations are well in hand for the ELEVENTH Sentinel Fun Run.

Nearly 700 runners, young and old, took part in the 1992 race - and next year's promises to be the biggest and best yet.

So watch your Sentinel for further details and entry form.

IT WAS a red-letter day for Wester Hailes on Friday September 4th, when local MP, Malcolm Rifkind, dropped in to help open a brand new housing development at Hailesland.

A Sentinel Special Report

The 97 homes are the Wester Hailes Community Housing Association's first major project - and they stand on the site formerly occupied by three high-rise blocks.

And according to one local woman the new houses are "a dream come true".

Mrs McWhirter who moved from Murrayburn with her three young children said:- The house is brilliant. The children can get out to play now which they couldn't before as we lived in a top floor flat."

Malcolm Rifkind, who paid a visit to Mrs McWhirter's home, was equally delighted with the development - especially the speed at which it had been done.

And he paid tribute to the work of the local people involved with the Housing Association. He said: "The hard work and efficiency of the Association has transformed this area and I am impressed by the quality of the design and finish of the new homes.

EFFORT

"And I must congratulate all concerned for their efforts in bringing the project to a successful completion."

Sheila Bunt, chairperson of the Housing Association said:- "It is hard to believe just how far we have come since we bought the land - complete with high-rise flats - from Edinburgh District Council.

"All the local people who have been involved have

worked extremely hard but it really is worthwhile when you look at the quality of the new homes and hear how pleased the first tenants are."

And another hard-working member of the Housing Association summed up everyone's feelings when he said he was "quietly satisfied" with the new development.

The Hailesland project cost £5 million pounds and was funded by Scottish Homes. The housing agency is also involved in the Association's next major house development in Westburn.

Work on that site is due to start at the end of September.

At the heart of the community

The Sentinel newspaper was first published in October 1976. It is now a fortnightly publication, distributed free to 10,000 households in Wester Hailes and the surrounding area.

Throughout its 16 - year history it has successfully campaigned on a variety of local issues, most notably housing and poverty.

The success of the Sentinel has led to the development of community newspapers throughout Edinburgh. And the city can now boast the strongest community news-paper sector in Europe.

Eight thousand, in fact, for six thousand homes. The planners had decided that Wester Hailes was to be a "dormitory suburb". The residents were to sleep in the estate – the rest of their life was to happen elsewhere.

What a vision! Thousands of people transported from the crumbling, Victorian tenements in Leith and other parts of city and abandoned on the west edge without the facilities to enable them to lead normal, fulfilled lives.

It was a recipe for urban disaster. But the human spirit is stronger than any planning nightmare. The doughty new residents bonded together in the face of their adversity and Wester Hailes began its long struggle to carve itself a place of pride in the city of Edinburgh. Tenants' associations were set up to articulate the miseries of living in sub-standard homes, voluntary organisations and self-help groups were formed to meet the social and recreational needs of the community. Community centres, affectionately known as "The Huts", were built from discarded classroom units.

'I'm getting severe hardship money just now anyway. It's alright. It's £23.90 a week'

'I'm quite proud of myself. I'll be eighteen in a couple of months and I haven't fell pregnant yet'

A local newspaper, the *Wester Hailes Sentinel,* was published to counteract the already negative image being portrayed in the Edinburgh press and money was scrounged from a variety of sources to support the ever burgeoning network of local groups. These groups were brought together under the umbrella of the Wester Hailes Representative Council. People entered the political process – they did not simply vote – they had their say as well. And what they said was: "We demand change".

A DAY IN THE LIFE

PERIPHERAL ESTATES

Paul Hunter

As well as Wester Hailes, there are two other districts of the city that are classed as areas of "multiple deprivation". They are Niddrie / Craigmillar in the east and Muirhouse / Pilton / West Granton to the north.

The majority of housing in the three schemes, including Wester Hailes, is owned by the public sector and collectively makes up 34 percent of Edinburgh District Council's housing stock. The areas all require major financial investment and suffer from a catalogue of problems, notably poor housing, high unemployment and poverty.

Although 45 percent of the housing stock in Niddrie/Craigmillar was built between 1946 and 1979, 54 percent of the homes were constructed between 1919 and 1945. Therefore it is simplistic and inaccurate to blame all its current difficulties on post-war planning mistakes. However, the bulk of Muirhouse/Pilton/West Granton appeared after the Second World War, with more than half being built between 1960 and 1979. In these cases charges of poor planning and the use of inferior building techniques and materials are more difficult to deny.

The estates have high rates of unemployment and associated low household income, with figures from January 1992 showing 28.5 percent of men in Craigmillar

Things have indeed changed since that first slab of concrete was put in place nearly a quarter of a century ago. The dreadful high-rise blocks have either been completely refurbished or are in the process of being emptied and demolished. New homes have been built and hundreds more are on the drawing board, and this time the people who are going to live in these new homes are in charge of the design. There is a shopping centre – not the most aesthetically pleasing building in the world, but there are plans, recession and the private sector willing, to breathe new life into it. There is now a police station, play parks, youth clubs, a secondary school, a health centre and a social club, there are even trees and shrubs where once there were only dog toilets. The public transport system is perhaps the best in

the city and those car parking spaces are slowly being transformed into colourful courtyards. But the estate's biggest asset is its people.

Thousands of people who refused to lie down meekly in the face of seemingly insurmountable hardship and political blindness, fought, schemed, bullied, begged, and demanded a better way of life, a better way of life that was enjoyed by most other people living in our beautiful city.

We have had some help of course. The guilty powers-to-be quickly recognised that Wester Hailes would be an unmitigated disaster in social and economic terms if they did not intervene, so over the years there has been a hotch-potch of initiatives, strategies and schemes to realise the potential of Wester Hailes. Everyone has got involved. The local authorities, the erstwhile Scottish Development Agency, academics, do-gooders, consultants by the score, and for several years now, central government has played a key role in trying to right the wrongs of the late sixties.

In 1989 the Scottish Office finally acknowledged the fact that 20 per cent of the Scottish people – one million souls – were living in dire poverty, and set up their "Partnership" projects.

Four estates were chosen as guinea-pigs for this long overdue exercise in urban renewal: Castlemilk in Glasgow, Dundee's Whitfield, Ferguslie Park in Paisley and Wester Hailes. Cynics have said that Wester Hailes was chosen because it was slap bang in the middle of then Scottish Secretary's Pentlands constituency but Malcolm

Rifkind had no need to buy votes in Wester Hailes. The estate was chosen because it suffered from all the indicators of chronic multiple deprivations: high unemployment, poor housing, no local economic base, social isolation and poverty. It was also chosen because the local residents had shown by their own endeavours that there was a solution to these problems – if the powers-to-be were willing to spend a little time, energy and hard cash.

Political prejudices and vested interests were set aside and everyone who is anyone in Scottish life sat round the table with the folk of Wester Hailes and set to work. A shared vision was hammered out and published in a glossy document entitled "Realising the Potential – a Partnership Strategy for Wester Hailes". Wester Hailes became an attractive,

receiving state benefits, while in Muirhouse the figure is 39 per cent. By comparison the Liberton ward, near Niddrie/Craigmillar has a male unemployment rate of 7.5 percent. And in the Willowbrae ward, which adjoins Muirhouse, the figure is 8.8 percent.

But all hope is not yet lost. Initiatives sponsored by the local authorities, the Scottish Office and the private sector are underway in an attempt to develop and renew the estates. Time alone will tell if these efforts will be fruitful, but some achievements, such as the refurbishment of housing stock, are already apparent.

The Pilton Partnership and the Craigmillar Festival Society are just two examples of bodies promoting the social, economic and physical regeneration of the areas they serve. These organisations and other local community groups are the catalysts for change and provide a sound basis for an optimistic future.

Further information can be had from:
Craigmillar Festival Society - Marjory Hawkes
(031) 661 5877
Pilton Partnership - John Mulvey
(031) 332 8472

A DAY IN THE LIFE

suburban town within Edinburgh participating fully in the social and economic life of the city with an active community and a well-developed local economy.

Targets were set to reduce the high unemployment, increase household income, to improve the housing stock and offer choice of tenure. The image of the estate was to be enhanced in the eyes of the rest of Edinburgh (with a particular eye on High Court judges perhaps). Wester Hailes was to become over the next decade, a place people wanted to move into – not an area where folk collected housing points in a desperate attempt to move out – and in time Wester Hailes would take its rightful place as part of Edinburgh, not a sink estate on the periphery. We were in short to come in from the cold.

By and large the Partnership is working – in spite of the challenges of a deep economic depression and restricted public spending. But in the midst of the euphoria of new *Brookside*-style housing, sophisticated marketing techniques and the Employment Service opening a new "one-stop" Job Centre, the enduring spectre of poverty cannot, and must not, be ignored.

Poverty is a an unpalatable fact of life in Wester Hailes and other similar areas throughout the city. It is also an uncomfortable truth that the statutory agencies and some local residents and groups cannot bring themselves to fully acknowledge. For many poverty is a dirty word.

It is no accident that the very first voluntary organisation set up in Wester Hailes way back in 1973 was **FISH** – **F**or **I**nformation and **S**ocial **H**elp. Its main aim was to help alleviate hardship among the elderly, the lonely and the disabled and it is perhaps a measure of how much still needs to be done, that 20 years later, FISH is still battling against the sometimes overwhelming tide of privation that many of our residents experience on a daily basis.

chip shop Spar post Ofice Paper shop

DIANE DUKE, PRIMARY 5

DONNA REDPATH, PRIMARY 5

'Wester Hailes - My Home'
by pupils of Sighthill
Primary School

'Most of my pals live here. I'm no wanting tae move cos I'd miss them all'

SHARLEEN SMITH, PRIMARY 6

ALAN POTTER, PRIMARY 6

KEVIN SCOTT, PRIMARY 2

'I got refused medical treatment - I had nausea, ken, wi ma heid getting bashed off the car. Got refused food, water and ma doctor and just slammed away up to court, like a piece of meat, ken what I mean? That's how they work; it's funny, that's how they work. It's hard to believe, you know what I mean if you dinnae stay here'

A DAY
IN THE
LIFE

6
WESTBURN GARDENS

'...I think they do try and do
a good job. I think they do
their best, they're not too bad'

A few months ago a young lad whose new flat had just been furnished with help from FISH, came into their office with his next door neighbour, a seventeen-year-old girl with a young baby. For six months she had been living in a flat in Wester Hailes with nothing but a duvet. She had no furniture, no cooking facilities, none of the ordinary paraphernalia that makes a home – all she had was a baby. Bare floorboards and a baby.

Her circumstances are thankfully somewhat extreme, but she is not alone in her poverty. A household survey conducted by the Scottish Office in 1989 showed that 80 per cent of the homes in Wester Hailes had an annual income of less than £10,000.

There has been nothing to indicate that this unacceptable level of financial hardship has been significantly alleviated in the last four years.

So alongside the dramatic physical and environmental changes that are taking place, much work still needs to be done to improve the economic prospects of local people. A daunting task, made all the worse by the current economic climate – and yet the one thing that Wester Hailes and its folk do not suffer from is poverty of spirit. It is the people's individual and collective courage and energy that has prevented the estate sinking into the despair and desolation that has overwhelmed many similar areas in Britain.

The people's enterprise and enthusiasm – their community spirit – has forced those in power to get off their backsides, roll up their shirt sleeves and muck in with a collective effort to fulfil the estate's potential. But there is still a long way to go. Only recently I happened to be at lunch with some of Edinburgh's establishment. The urbane gentleman next to me leant over and enquired politely where I lived. 'Wester Hailes,' said I. 'How brave,' was his astonishing, but sadly not untypical, reply.

No sir, I am not brave. I am privileged. I live in an area where folk look after their own, where collective action is a reality and not an empty political slogan. I live in an area that has a sense of destiny and pride and I for one wouldn't live anywhere else.

'I think the council have let the condition of the housing drop dramatically'

'Well, I must say I have got a lovely clean stair. There's never a mark on it. Spotless, not a bit of writing on it or nothing. It's great'

THE ATHENS OF THE NORTH

NICHOLAS PHILLIPSON

Nicholas Phillipson is Reader in History
at Edinburgh University, and a specialist in
the history of the Scottish Enlightenment.
He is author of *Hume* (Weidenfeld and Nicolson, 1989)
and many articles on the Scottish Enlightenment.
He was educated at Aberdeen and Cambridge Universities
and has had several visiting university appointments
in America. He is currently a member of the Council of the
Edinburgh International Festival.

'What is
so interesting,
historically, is that
this public comes
from exactly the same
social world as the
one which made the
Enlightenment
possible'

*'Pompous
the boast,
and yet the
truth it speaks.
A "Modern Athens",
- fit for modern
Greeks'*

JAMES HANNAY

For the past two centuries, high culture has played a crucial and curious part in shaping Edinburgh's history and providing her with a sense of identity. Two centuries ago the city was one of the major Centres of Enlightenment in the western world, "*a hot-bed of genius*" as Tobias Smollett's Mathew Bramble put it. Edinburgh rejoiced in an intelligentsia whose reputation for philosophy, history and the natural sciences and for literature, architecture and the visual arts led some of the local literati to liken Edinburgh to Periclean Athens and to think of it as the Athens of the North. This was not a bad tag for a city which was associated with the philosopher David Hume, the historians William Robertson and Adam Ferguson, and those remarkable natural scientists, Joseph Black and James Hutton, nor was it inappropriate for a city whose university was one of the most admired and emulated in the western world. The tag became even more popular in the early nineteenth century during the age of Sir Walter Scott and that most influential of nineteenth-century journals, the *Edinburgh Review*. But although the city has never been able to maintain the extraordinary level of intellectual achievement it reached during the age of Enlightenment, the Athenian tag has stuck, fixing the image of Edinburgh as a city of culture in the eyes of the world. It would probably have withered and died by now, had it not been for the Edinburgh International Festival which was founded in 1947 in order to celebrate and encourage excellence in the performing and visual arts. It's clear from tourist industry reports that the Festival has now become as important to the city's international reputation and to its sense of identity - not to mention its economy - as the Enlightenment ever was, giving new life to the old Athenian imagery. And although Edinburgh's reputation as the Athens of the North now has more to do with the arts and less to do with learning and literature than it did during the Enlightenment, it is still bound up with the pursuit of high culture, to the considerable embarrassment of a few local patriots who are proud of the city's Athenian reputation but distrust the élitism and the cosmopolitanism with which it seems to be associated. Understanding Edinburgh, therefore, means understanding

its culture and the historical circumstances that shaped it. And when we understand that, we shall understand the importance of being a modern Athens.

Edinburgh's emergence as an important centre of enlightenment during the eighteenth century is not at all easy to explain. Some historians think that it was the result of a long evolutionary process which had begun in the sixteenth century when Scotland was still an independent state and Edinburgh was a royal city. This was a period when the city generated a vigorous court culture which soon became interwoven with the Presbyterianism of the Scottish reformers. It was a cosmopolitan, humanist culture which looked to ancient Greece and Rome and to modern Europe for inspiration and set out to show how the arts and sciences could be used to teach kings, counsellors, clergy and gentlemen how to serve the public in a modern Presbyterian state. But this noble, if somewhat conventional, classical ideal was soon dissipated by the pressure of political and religious events. In 1603, James VI succeeded to the English throne, the court left Edinburgh and moved to London. What is more, bitter sectarian quarrels within the Kirk spilled over into the university, encouraging the nobility and gentry to send their children to the celebrated Dutch universities for their higher education. Edinburgh's cultural fortunes flagged, and it was not until the later seventeenth century that there were any real signs of a revival. Doctors, lawyers and men of letters who had been educated in London or Holland began to set up clubs and societies in the city for encouraging the arts and sciences and looked for private tutors who could teach law, medicine and the classics in the Dutch manner to those who could not afford to spend time in the Low Countries. It was a modest revival of the old patriotic and patrician humanist ideal of a culture which linked the arts and sciences to public life and helped to create a well-educated, modern-minded political élite.

Some historians see these developments as the building blocks on which the remarkable cultural achievements of the eighteenth century were raised - and so, in a sense, they were. For one of the most striking characteristics of Edinburgh's enlightened literati was their humanistic belief in the importance of learning and literature to public life. University professors like William Robertson, Adam Ferguson and Joseph Black attached enormous importance to the fact that they were training up students who were destined for careers in the Kirk and in public life. David Hume - surely the greatest Scottish philosopher and historian - and Walter Scott both wrote in different ways about the extraordinary transformations through which the modern world was passing so that they could help their fellow citizens to adapt to a world which was radically different and often uncomfortably unfamiliar to the one their parents and grandparents had known. And all of these formidable intellectuals inhabited a city of clubs and societies which met in the salons, coffee-houses and taverns and where they discussed philosophy, science and literature and the improvement of contemporary society over dinner and sometimes a great deal of drink (it was no wonder that the *literati* were sometimes known as the *eaterati*). These ideals not only had roots in an earlier period of Edinburgh's history - they also had much in common with those of enlightened

JOHN NAPIER, 1550-1617

From Edinburgh but went to the University of St. Andrews. In 1588 became Commissioner to the General Assembly. Took 20 years to construct the table of logarithms for which he is best remembered, called Rabdologiae. Napier University named after him.

ALEXANDER GRAHAM BELL 1847-1922

Patented telephone in 1876

Alexander Graham Bell with his wife.
(Edinburgh Central Library)

EDINBURGH UNIVERSITY

Edinburgh University was founded in 1583 by the city under the charter granted the previous year by King James VI of Scotland. It was both the first civic and first post-Reformation university in Britain and the addition of Edinburgh, as the most modern of Scotland's four ancient universities, meant that for the next 250 years, Scotland had four institutions of higher education, while England had only two.

The "Town's college" of Edinburgh prospered in that time. By the 18th century Medicine and Law complemented the founding disciplines of Arts and Divinity and the University of Edinburgh, at the centre of the Scottish Enlightenment, had become one of the leading universities of the Western World. In the l9th century Music and Science were added to its fields of study and in the 20th Veterinary Medicine and Social Science.

1789 saw the start of a rebuilding programme, which was to result in the completion of the present Old College, to designs by Robert Adam and William Playfair. Since then the University has expanded to precincts across Edinburgh, making it truly "the university in the city".

The roll call of those who have studied or taught at the University of Edinburgh is a long and distinguished one - including James Boswell and Oliver Goldsmith, Charles Darwin, Joseph Lister and James Simpson, David Hume, Walter Scott and Thomas Carlyle, Robert Louis Stevenson and Arthur Conan Doyle. Currently a number of leading political figures, such as Malcolm Rifkind, David Steel and Gordon Brown, number among the University's alumni.

Now with nearly 11,000 undergraduates and 3,500 postgraduates spread across its eight faculties, Edinburgh is one of the largest universities in Britain, with a flexible degree structure offering a wide range of choice within the Scottish 4-year system. It is also a international centre, with students drawn from nearly 100 different countries. A major focus for postgraduate study and research, the University currently handles over £38m annually in research grants and contracts from the Research Councils, Government, industry and commerce, and the European Community. Its research ratings make it the leading research university in Scotland.

While conscious of its history, however, the University of Edinburgh's sights are set firmly on the future, and it thus maintains its emphasis on innovation. Edinburgh founded the first UK Chairs of English Literature and Agriculture and it is presently well represented among:

• the hi-tech disciplines such as Artificial Intelligence where it has the leading university department in Europe;

• international relations based on units including its distinguished Europa Centre and

• languages and area studies where it offers one of the broadest range of choices across European, Middle and Far Eastern studies.

The University is also a major academic and international centre for computing, with the most powerful supercomputer in the UK, the 16,384 processor Connection Machine, sited in Edinburgh's Parallel Computing Centre.

communities everywhere. Cities like Dublin, Boston, Copenhagen, Toulouse and Naples all had their societies of men of letters who belonged to the gentry and to the professional and commercial classes and were interested in learning and public life. What is so striking about the enlightened culture of Edinburgh was not its ideals but the exceptional intellectual creativity which they generated. The philosophical histories of Hume, Ferguson and Robertson helped to create an entirely new type of historical writing which explored the social and economic fabric of human civilisation in ways which still influence our historical thinking. Black and Hutton wrought a similar transformation in thinking about the organisation of the natural world. Scott discovered ways of using fiction as a vehicle of historical writing and a whole generation revolutionised the history of the media by bringing into existence new forms of journalism. So why was it that Edinburgh, rather than Dublin or Copenhagen or Boston, became the Northern Athens?

Part of the answer lies in an extraordinary historical accident. Edinburgh was fortunate enough to have a gregarious and much-loved genius among its citizens. David Hume, who was born in 1711 and died in 1776, was not only one of the most profound and delightful of philosophers but a sceptic whose philosophy exposed the perilously shaky intellectual foundations on which contemporary thinking about religion, politics and science rested. His message was that human beings could only find true happiness if they abandoned outworn dogmas and learned to be adaptable and pragmatic in their outlook. Hume exercised the most profound influence on the intellectual life of Edinburgh - and, indeed, of Scotland. Although he was a notorious religious sceptic, his philosophy and his conversation encouraged intelligent Christians to think again about the foundations on which their faith was built; it provoked questions about the nature and purpose of government in a modern commercial state and it played a crucial part in laying the foundations of what would soon be known as the science of political economy. Natural scientists found that his philosophy had provoked important scientific questions which deserved serious answers. And it is often forgotten that Sir Walter Scott's understanding of history was profoundly influenced by Hume's remarkable *History of England.* For one of the most striking characteristics of Edinburgh's culture was that the Edinburgh literati took Hume's philosophy seriously and realised that it offered intellectual challenges which had to be addressed by an intelligentsia that believed that learning mattered politically. But Hume only mattered to Edinburgh because the city already had a sophisticated and intelligent élite which was able to make the most of him. Why was this so? Contemporaries thought that the answer was to be found in the extraordinary changes which had taken place in Scotland since the Glorious Revolution of 1688. They thought that the restoration of Presbyterianism in 1690 had provided a new opportunity to turn Scotland into a Presbyterian polity and that the Act of Union of 1707 had provided the country with new opportunities for creating political stability and for generating economic growth. These opportunities had of course not come free, and Edinburgh's citizens often ruefully reflected on the loss of status that the

JAMES HUTTON 1726-1797
"Father of modern geology."
Studied medicine at Edinburgh
University. Wrote *Theory of the Earth*
in 1785 - the foundation for modern
geological theory.

VISCOUNT STAIR 1619-1695
Judge. Wrote *Institutions of the Law*
***of Scotland* in 1681, which codified**
Scots law into a coherent system for
the first time.

Sir Walter Scott. *(Edinburgh Central Library)*

DAVID HUME 1711-1776

Scotland's greatest philosopher.

Wrote *Treatise of Human Nature* -

his first and greatest work. It was an

attempt to introduce the experimental

method of reasoning into moral

subjects.

city had suffered with the abolition of the old Scots parliament and the departure of the nobility for London. On the other hand, they now had it in their power to turn Scotland into a prosperous, Presbyterian polity within the framework of a powerful, modern British state, and they knew it. It was a situation that encouraged them to to go back to fundamentals, and to think about the role of religion, law and government, and that in turn encouraged them to think again critically and freshly about the principles of theology, jurisprudence and politics and about human nature itself. In other words, they came to think of learning and letters as a machine for modernising an underdeveloped country. All of this made them acute critics of existing ways of thinking about man, society and nature and gave them a remarkable insight into the mechanisms which controlled the progress of society from its "rude" to its "refined" states.

　　And it made them equally acute critics of English politics - for here was a country which was rapidly becoming one of the most wealthy and powerful states in the world and which had a constitution which was one of the political wonders

of the modern world, yet its public life was dominated by corrupt and factious party politicians who spent their time in party infighting and in squabbling about yesterday's ideologies. They (the English) seemed to have no idea of how to manage the affairs of an advanced commercial state! This was one of the reasons which encouraged the literati to think of Edinburgh as a modern Athens or, as someone once put it, the "*Athens of Britain*." Athenian culture, linking learning to public life, had been the glory of the ancient world. But, as everyone knew, Athens had lost its independence and had become a province of imperial Rome; thereafter, its destiny had been to supply the new empire with the political and moral wisdom its rulers had so conspicuously lacked. The history of Athens had shown that culture could become a substitute for sovereignty.

　　Throughout the nineteenth century, Edinburgh remained the same sort of city that it had been during the Enlightenment: a literate, professional and

'Of my
boyhood,
I need say that it
was spartan at home
and more spartan
at school where a
tawse-brandishing
schoolmaster of the
old type made
our young lives
miserable'

**SIR ARTHUR
CONAN-DOYLE**

commercial city with a fairly large and reputable university, a respectable literary life and a significant publishing industry. It was a patrician city, self-conscious about its status, which still hung on to its Athenian image at a time when Glasgow was rapidly emerging as one of the workshops of Victorian Britain. But enlightenments need exceptional intellectual talent as well as social structures and institutions to support them - and that is what Victorian Edinburgh lacked. Perhaps inevitably, the university fell into the hands of professors who had more interest in perpetuating increasingly old-fashioned enlightened traditions of teaching and research than in taking stock of new ones and it soon found itself outclassed by Oxbridge and the German universities. The literary world seemed content to breed *petits maitres* cast in the mould of Scott and the journalists of his age. Perhaps most telling of all, talented Scots like James Mill and Thomas Carlyle, who wanted to exploit the revolution in economic and historical thinking that had taken place during the Enlightenment, found it was now more congenial to do so in London.

An insidious nostalgia began to infect the city. To contemporaries it seemed that the progress of commerce, the improvement of communications, the spread of government and Anglicisation was eroding Edinburgh's special status. Scotland, said Scott, was in danger of becoming "*an inferior species of Northumberland*". The Enlightenment, that civilised and sensible antiquary Henry Cockburn commented, had belonged to "*the last purely Scotch Age*". In their efforts to perpetuate the culture of the Enlightenment, the literati of Victorian Edinburgh had fallen into the very trap from which their enlightened forebears had tried to save them. They had forgotten Hume's dictum that, in the modern world, human happiness goes hand in hand with adaptability, and that progress depends on a society's ability to distance itself from tradition and to generate new cultures to articulate its rapidly-changing needs. If Edinburgh was ever to put new wind in its Athenian sails it would have to find new sources of inspiration and new institutions to do it and that did not happen until 1947.

Culture often thrives on crisis and Edinburgh's has been no exception. It is hard to see how it could have developed as an enlightened city without the transforming effects of the religious and political upheavals of the late seventeenth and early eighteenth centuries on the attitudes of its élite. It's even harder to see how it could have developed as a Festival city without the Second World War. The war had numbed the arts in Europe. Orchestras, opera, ballet and theatre companies had been dismantled or put into cold storage. International contacts between artists had been virtually impossible. The Lord Provost and the small group of citizens who founded the Edinburgh International Festival in 1947 hoped that an annual festival in Edinburgh would help to revive the arts in Europe as well as in Scotland and that it would help to put Edinburgh on the international map as a modern city of culture. Its success in doing so in the early days is legendary. The fact that it is still the world's largest festival of the performing arts testifies to its continuing and unique standing in the international arts world and helps to explain the extraordinary proliferation of festivals that cluster round the

'Here it was that the Ursa Major of literature stayed for a few days, in 1773, and did receive the homage of the trembling literati of Edinburgh'

ROBERT CHAMBERS ON DR. JOHNSON

HERIOT-WATT UNIVERSITY

Heriot-Watt University, Edinburgh, is a modern technologically-based university particularly known for its range of technological, professional and vocational courses, providing a stimulating educational environment for producing skills which are in consistently high demand among employers, its long-standing relationship with industry, commerce and the professions in providing training and research of direct economic benefit and social relevance, fostering innovation and supporting internationally regarded programmes of research its Research Park, which was the first of its kind in the UK, now recognised as an exemplary academic-commercial development; its centres of excellence in offshore and petroleum engineering, marine technology and environmental issues; optoelectronics; information technology (including the pioneering developments of the Institute for Computer-Based Learning); the unique International Centre for Brewing and Distilling; the Institute of Technology Management; and the International Centre for Island Technology.

The university's main campus is at Riccarton in west Edinburgh, where the major capital development programme completed in 1992 has created the most up-to-date facilities in UK higher education, in an unspoilt natural setting.

Riccarton Campus houses the Faculties of Science, Engineering and Economic & Social Studies (including the Heriot-Watt Business School). Purpose-built academic facilities are supported by intensive computing, information and library services, as well as residential, catering, recreational and sporting amenities. There are some 1,000 residential places on the campus and accommodation is virtually guaranteed to first year students from outside the Edinburgh locality.

The university's Faculties of Environmental Studies and Art & Design at Edinburgh College of Art, the Institute of Education at Moray House College, and the Faculty of Textiles at the Scottish College of Textiles are located on their own campus sites.

The university's six faculties and Institute of Education have approximately 8,000 students, of whom around 1,500 are postgraduates, taught by over 700 academic staff. Some 15 per cent of students are from overseas, representing 80 different nations.

Edinburgh International Festival during the summer. For August is also the month of the Film Festival, the Television Festival, the Jazz Festival, the Tattoo and, above all, that rumbustious, anarchic and often potent celebration of shamateurism, the Fringe. It is the month when great companies and their audiences are mobile and internationally-minded. It is the month when Edinburgh's tourist trade is at its height and the city is best able to recharge its Athenian batteries.

The Festival seems to flourish for the same reasons as the Enlightenment did in the eighteenth century. Its director, who is and has to be something of a cultural autocrat during his term of office, is its David Hume. He is the source of its inspiration, the sole architect of its programmes, the father of its fortunes. This has made some commentators wonder whether these annual celebrations of high culture are not simply one-man shows which have more to do with promoting the tourist industry than with the city's culture. But that can't be so; for one thing, about half of the tickets are still bought by Edinburgh citizens. What is so interesting,

'In November 1789 we got a half holiday to see the foundation stone of the new college laid, which was done with great civic and masonic pomp'

LORD COCKBURN

Laying the foundation stone, University of Edinburgh, 1789. *(Edinburgh Central Library)*

historically, is that this public comes from exactly the same social world as the one which made the Enlightenment possible; the world of the professions and commerce, the world which continues to dominate the economy and public life of the city. But whereas the professional and commercial world of the Enlightenment was oligarchic and exclusive in character, that of modern Edinburgh is far more complex in character and has a far broader social base. Its professional sector and the service industries that support it employ almost two thirds of the working population and dovetails with the student subculture which clusters round the city's universities. It is a society which continues to enjoy high culture in an informal and unstuffy way, realising that it is exciting and fun and that it provides the city with a reputation, an identity and a healthy tourist industry. It is an attitude which has restored and rehabilitated Edinburgh's claim to truly be the *Athens of the North.*

NAPIER UNIVERSITY

Napier is one of the largest universities in Scotland, with 9,100 students of whom 5,600 are engaged in full-time study.

Napier University takes its name from John Napier, inventor of logarithms, who was born in the Tower of Merchiston in 1550 The Tower, restored and refurbished, is part of Merchiston campus, the original Napier College of Science and Technology which opened in 1964.

In 1974 the College merged with the Edinburgh College of Commerce, situated at Sighthill, forming Napier College of Commerce and Technology.

Since then Napier has expanded steadily into centres at Craiglockart, Marchmont, Redwood House and North Merchiston. In 1988, in recognition of its achievements, the College became Napier Polytechnic of Edinburgh and in June 1992 Napier was given consent by the Privy Council to adopt the title "Napier University".

All Napier's buildings are on the west side of Edinburgh and within easy reach of each other by public transport as well as by an inter-campus mini-bus service.

Napier's proximity to Scotland's industrial heartland, and in particular to 'Silicon Glen', has assisted its policy of close collaboration with industry and in providing opportunities for integrating study and work experience.

Napier's four faculties of Applied Art, Engineering, the Napier Business School and Science offer opportunities for study and research in a wide variety of areas and a full range of vocationally oriented courses is offered not only at degree level, undergraduate and post-graduate, but at certificate and Higher National Diploma level.

Napier offers courses which are geared towards the world of work, they are designed in collaboration with industry and business and many of them involve a period a supervised work experience as an integrated part of the course.

An advantage of the kind of course offered at Napier is the facility for students to 'articulate' or progress from certificate and diploma courses onto degree and postgraduate courses. A student can start on a Higher National Diploma course and, depending on his or her rate of progress, often transfer to a degree course in the same subject area. This allows an entry to Higher Education to students with a wide range of abilities and attainments and is one of the keys to increasing the numbers of young people participating in Higher Education.

All Napier's departments are engaged actively in applied research and consultancy and in 1988 Polyed (Napier Consultancy Services) was set up as the interface between the business community and the range of services and resources offered by academic departments. Particular areas of expertise include: Computer Aided Engineering, Transportation Engineering, Polymer Technology and Industrial Design.

Napier's ethos makes it the ideal vehicle for both educating tomorrow's managers, engineers and scientists and for providing a training, research and consultancy resource for industry and commerce in today's competitive world.

*'I have
no space left
to enlarge on
the friendliness
and hospitality
with which
the visitor
to Edinburgh
is greeted'*

E. M. FORSTER

Jean Jacques Rousseau. *Allan Ramsay (National Gallery of Scotland)*

SPORTING EDINBURGH

IAN WOOD

Ian Wood is golf correspondent and regular columnist with *The Scotsman,* after a career with that newspaper spanning three decades. He went into journalism after finishing his National Service in Cyprus with the Royal Signals.
Combining sub-editing with sports writing, he was appointed sports editor in 1975, a post he held for eleven years until making the transition to full-time writing.

'The stadium at Meadowbank, at which were staged the Commonwealth Games of 1970 and 1986, generated its share of the heat...'

One of the attractions of Musselburgh race days in the years immediately preceding the Second World War, was a large West Indian who used to set up his stall near the Town Hall. His props consisted of a chair and a bucket of hot water and his speciality was yanking troublesome teeth out of the heads of suffering punters with his bare hands.

Dental Health then was not what it is today and he did a roaring trade - screaming, might be nearer the mark - at a shilling per extraction. He was, apparently, skilled in his art and, of course, hygiene was of the highest order - hence, the bucket.

This story is recalled merely to point up the spin-off effects of sporting events on communities generally and, in this instance, on Edinburgh life in particular. Not that Musselburgh would ever submit to being lumped in with Edinburgh in the normal way of things, but, perhaps, as the venue for what are nationally referred to as Edinburgh's race meetings, the Honest Toun will allow an exception here.

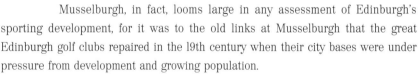

Musselburgh, in fact, looms large in any assessment of Edinburgh's sporting development, for it was to the old links at Musselburgh that the great Edinburgh golf clubs repaired in the l9th century when their city bases were under pressure from development and growing population.

In the fullness of time, the societies of the Royal Burgess and Bruntsfield Links returned to Edinburgh and their present homes, the Honourable Company of Edinburgh Golfers having soldiered along the coast to Muirfield. The Royal Musselburgh club finally moved to Prestongrange and the old Musselburgh nine-hole course was left to its own devices within the racecourse. It continues stubbornly to survive, in spite of recent savaging in the interests of National Hunt racing.

It's an ill wind, however, and while the development of racing "over the jumps" took a bite out of the old links - a bit of a liberty really, for the course had

spawned five Open Champions - it brought to the racing scene a new dimension, adding an all-year, all-weather facility. The Edinburgh meetings remain an established popular feature of Scottish sporting life, even if the crowds are not quite what they were in the days when cut-price dentistry was thrown in.

Fewer people now watch the traditional "major" sports - international rugby and professional football - mainly because the capacities of stadia have been drastically reduced in the pursuit of safety and comfort. Murrayfield, home of the Scottish Rugby Union and the national team, has been transformed in the course of some 15 years from a starkly basic place comprising one stand and vast terracing to an imposing, streamlined stadium of soaring stands and corporate ticket allocations.

The price of this beautification - apart from the projected £47 million - is that where once getting on for 100,000 people could and did cram into the old ground, the capacity of the new Murrayfield is around 50,000, the two remaining open terraces and the replacement of the original stand will have converted the ground into a huge two-tier bowl with everybody seated under one roof.

There have been, along the way, whines from the grass-roots following, some of whom have been finding it difficult to get tickets to watch the show pieces of the game they play or support on a weekly basis, but then, you can't have everything. If they ever do get a ticket, at least they can luxuriate in the surroundings befitting a great sporting spectacle. Whether followers of Hearts or Hibs will be as lucky remains to be seen.

W.S. Gilbert wrote of a time when *"every boy and every girl born into this world alive was either a little Liberal or else a little Conservative"*. In Edinburgh it is rather like that in terms of being born into and under the influence of either Hearts or Hibs. The rivalry between the two factions has never been quite so all-consuming as that which prevails in Glasgow between Rangers and Celtic, and there was a time, not that long ago, before people started to go mad, when games between Hearts and Hibs could be attended in a spirit of amiable banter. However, whether in that gentler era, or in this demented one, the rivalry has always been deep-seated and intense and, indeed, lends no little savour to the football scene in the capital. The mood on Saturday evenings in many households throughout the city is dictated by the respective fates of Hearts and Hibs that afternoon. The office on a Monday morning can be a place of light and joy for those whose team has been successful, Hell on earth, for those whose team has failed.

For both clubs things are not quite what they used to be. Both had their heydays in the fifties and though there have been good moments and pleasing seasons since, it has been a long time since 48,000 watched Hearts at Tynecastle and 54,000 watched Hibs at Easter Road, the latter record standing before Hibs built a towering extension to their terracing in the hope that the boom years would go on (which they didn't!).

That Easter Road extension has long since gone and the ground is more or less as it was in those early days. So is Tynecastle. There have been cosmetic

'Edinburgh has been happily compared with a flag – a thing of history, worn and stained with old deeds and great days, and starred with burning names'

ALANSON B. HAUGHTON

changes here and there, but both grounds are little more than tatty reminders of better days. It is high time for a change but the indications are that it's not going to be easy.

The same depth of feeling which has enabled the clubs to feed off each other over the years, is not helping now that a new and unprecedented situation has to be faced. With the talk of super leagues and the influence of big business ever more in evidence, something clearly has to be done in order to get decks cleared economically and ground-sharing is an obvious first step.

So far, the signs are not promising. An approach in 1991 by Hearts was interpreted by the Hibs support as cover for a take-over and that was that. Since then, the Easter Road club have declared themselves sympathetic to combined action to build a common stadium, but this time the Hearts were dismissive and determined to go their own way.

As things stand at present, Hibs have their sights trained on one location, Hearts have theirs on another. With the stage set for two new grounds which will strain the resources of both clubs, the local authorities are trying to steer the two towards a possible scheme for a shared stadium at Ingliston, where the Highland Show people have space and are willing to talk terms. The prospect of one stadium for the price of two has so much going for it, the chances of it coming to pass must be classed as slight.

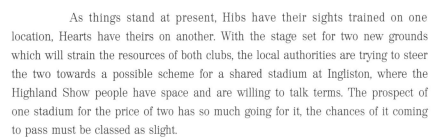

The stadium at Meadowbank, at which were staged the Commonwealth Games of 1970 and 1986, generated its share of heat when it was being built, the phrase "white elephant" being bandied about with some abandon. It would be interesting to know what the youngsters - and not a few oldsters - who go along to the sports centre to avail themselves of its many facilities would say to that.

As to the Commonwealth Games, the 1970 event was an unqualified success thanks in no small measure to the skilled organisational hand of the late

ERIC LIDDELL.
Athlete. In July 1923 he broke the 100 yards British record. He won the gold medal at the Paris Olympics of 1924 in the 440 yards but refused to take part in the 100 yards heats because they were being held on a Sunday. Died in 1945 in a Japanese prison camp.

ALLAN WELLS
Athlete. Born 1953. At the Moscow Olympics of 1980, he won the 100m gold medal in 10.25 seconds.

KEN BUCHANAN
Boxer. World Lightweight Champion 1970-1973. One of Scotland's greatest boxing heroes, conspicuous in his tartan shorts!

TOMMY ARMOUR
Golfer known as "The Silver Scot". He won the US Open, the US PGA and the British Open in 1924 and the US PGA again in 1930, as well as the US Open and British Open in 1931. One of Scotland's greatest golfers.

Robert Forman, a former PT teacher at the Royal High School. Life in the "village" was harmony itself and, as if all that was not enough, Scotland's own Lachie Stewart beat the legendary Ron Clarke in the 10,000 metres. So moved was Lachie at outrunning his hero, he said he was sorry. The Australian indicated that he wasn't too happy either.

Next time round, in 1986, the Games had a rather more rocky progress. We had, by then, entered the age of the political boycott and 30 countries out of the original entry of 58 backed out over the British Government's policy on sanctions against South Africa. There was a financial crisis which was resolved when Robert Maxwell arrived like the Seventh Cavalry, or at least we thought the crisis had been resolved. There are those who remain unconvinced to this day. The one certain thing is that Maxwell arrived and his last act at the Games was when, during the farewell march-past of competitors, he dashed to the track to help replace the Scottish contingent's Saltire which had fallen, rather symbolically, from its flagpole.

On top of all this, it rained heavily and practically without pause. Astonishingly, the crowd remained in good heart and at the ready and, having warmed up with a few Mexican waves, they cheered Liz McColgan all the way as she ground down the opposition to win the 10,000 metres.

Meadowbank also houses the Skol Sprint, which has, over the years, featured runners such as Tranent's George McNeil, whose recognition as one of the world"s fastest men was blurred by the professional tag which seems so irrelevant when few stars do anything for nothing. The sprint moved to Meadowbank from Powderhall, where the greyhounds race and which is home to the Edinburgh Monarchs speedway team who, confusingly, used to work their wonders at Old Meadowbank, site of the present stadium.

While at Powderhall, the sprint, held over the New Year holiday, built up the international reputation it enjoys today and the popularity of the event can be gauged from the fact that when one W. Haddock, of Stockton-on-Tees, won in 1914, a crowd of 18,000 was on hand to see him do it.

The speedway team are hardly drawing this sort of support, but then this has always tended to be a sport of fluctuating popularity. It enjoyed one of its peaks in the fifties, when Jack Young, the World Champion, was the main attraction and the crowds filled Old Meadowbank. Things are somewhat muted right now and the recession is having its effects, speedway being vulnerable to fuel, rider and machine costs.

However, if speedway seems to come and go, it generally manages to survive, and the Monarchs, whose present crop of stars includes a home-grown Scot, Kenny McKinna, and the Englishmen, Les Collins and Michael Coles, are well geared to do that. They languish presently in the lower reaches of Division II, but they have in their manager, Alan Bridgett, a man with a feel for success, having enjoyed it himself with the Monarchs in the eighties when, as a rider, he helped them win the Knock-Out Cup and the National Fours Tournament.

Swimmers in Edinburgh are well catered for, the principal centre being the Commonwealth Pool, which served the Games, a striking award-winning design, to which youngsters flock inspired perhaps, by the deeds of David Wilkie, the man from the Warrender club, whose victory in the 200 metres breaststroke at the 1976 Montreal Olympics made him the first British male swimmer to take gold in 60 years.

Portobello once led the way, with its open-air pool (now, alas gone, artificial waves and all) and its baths where the Channel swimmer, Ned Barnie, used to confound gala spectators by diving from the gallery rail into the shallow end. The baths then were salt water, which, for many people, gave them an edge over other indoor pools. Once the tanks and pipes gave out, it was, apparently, impossible to replace them. So much for space-age technology.

Ice-hockey aficionados follow the fortunes of Murrayfield Racers at the ice-rink which is situated about a well-struck puck away from the rugby stadium. The Racers are Britain's most successful hockey side, having won more tournaments than any other. Since their last major success, however - they won the premier league in season 1986-87 - they have been going through an increasingly lean spell.

The last three seasons have been particularly poor and, indeed, things got so bad that Robert Adams, an Edinburgh businessman and devoted Racers follower, couldn't stand it any longer and bought the team in the summer of 1991. He and his brother-in-law, Derek Reilly, a former Racer who scored more than 1,000 goals for the club, now stand ready to restore good order and good times at Murrayfield, where one of the attractions is Tony Hand, generally regarded as British hockey's best home-bred player.

RICHARD NOBLE
Driver. Born in 1946, he took the World Land Speed Record on October 4th 1983 in the Nevada desert at 638 mph in his car 'Thrust 2'.

ANDY IRVINE
Rugby Player. Played for Scotland from 1972-1982 and won 51 Scottish caps scoring over 250 points for Scotland. He was the most exciting and lethal attacking full-back of his generation.

MARTIN BELL
Skier. He is Britain's top Alpine skier.

DAVID WILKIE
Swimmer. He won 15 major swimming medals including 8 gold in major games. He took 30 major records - 3 World, 9 European and 18 Commonwealth. He was never beaten in the 200m breaststroke from September 1973 till his retirement in 1976 and won the gold medal in the Montreal Olympics of 1976.

*'The
weather is raw
and boisterous
in winter, shifty and
ungenial in summer
and downright
meteorological
purgatory in
the spring'*

**ROBERT LOUIS
STEVENSON**

WHO
LOVES THE
FESTIVAL?

CLIVE SANDGROUND

Journalist and broadcaster
Clive Sandground is a former editor
of the *Scottish Daily Express* and the *Sunday Mail,*
and was one of the launch team
of the *Sunday Standard* before joining
the Edinburgh International Festival
as head of publicity in 1984
- a position he held until 1991.

*'Glasgow was
chosen to be
European Capital
of Culture for one
year. Edinburgh is
the World's Capital
of Culture in
perpetuity'*

Edinburgh is the most gloriously beautiful city on earth, particularly during August when it is en fete. And yet, looking at it logically, isn't it the last place you would expect to find the world's largest arts jamboree?

As the crusty but much-loved maestro Sir Thomas Beecham said in the early days: "It is madness to expect Edinburgh to host a festival when it is too mean to fund the building of decent venues."

Nearly half a century on, things must be changing.

Yet the Edinburgh Festival is still here, growing ever larger year by year. The Festival, with its half-dozen concurrent satellites (Festival Fringe, Military Tattoo, and Film, Jazz, Book and Television Festivals) now doubles the city's population every August as visitors, performers, administrators and critics pour in from around the globe.

I fell passionately in love with Edinburgh during that first Festival in the long hot summer of 1947 when, as a 14-year-old schoolboy, I came here on holiday from the west of Scotland.

The war may have been over, but Britain still lived frugally. Most things were either rationed or in short supply. And although the blackout curtains had long been taken down, our cities were still pretty gloomy places, with dim street lights and darkened shop windows. And then I discovered Edinburgh.

Walking out of the old Princes Street Station (it stood on what is now the Caledonian Hotel's car park) into the hot summer night was a magical experience. Everywhere there was light, laughter and colour - and to hell with austerity. The Princes Street windows were ablaze; the Castle was floodlit; the tramcars were all bedecked from stem to stern with flags and bunting. And the streets were thronged with happy, noisy, excited people, chattering in a dozen languages as they bustled to and from theatres, concert halls, pubs and clubs.

My young life had never experienced anything like this before. Wow! What a way to celebrate the end of the war.

But this was no mere victory celebration; there was no triumphalism. The Festival brought together, in friendship and music, the war-ravaged peoples of the world. The 1947 opening concert in the Usher Hall embodied that spirit - when maestro Bruno Walter, driven from his homeland by Nazi persecution, was emotionally reunited with his beloved Vienna Philharmonic Orchestra, many of whose musicians had also suffered.

The Director of that first Festival was another Austrian, Rudolf Bing, who ran the Glyndebourne Opera in Sussex.

But Bing alone could not have foisted his Festival on to the people of Edinburgh, particularly as there was much scepticism among the ranks of the City Council, dour, cautious, grey men cast in the municipal mould. But Edinburgh has always been blessed by her men of vision - a number of whom gave Bing the support he needed to overcome the doubters.

Foremost among these was Harvey Wood, who represented Scotland on the British Council; Sir John Falconer, the city's Lord Provost; Murray Watson, the editor of the *Scotsman*, and John Cameron QC, who was later to become one of Scotland's foremost judges.

Rudolf Bing ran the Festival until 1949 before taking over the Metropolitan Opera in New York. Happily he is still alive, as is Lord Cameron.

After Bing's departure, his deputy, Ian Hunter, took up the reins, to be followed in turn by Robert Ponsonby, Lord Harewood, Peter Diamand, John Drummond, Frank Dunlop, and the current Festival Director, Brian McMaster.

I suspect that most of them - if not all - had reason to be grateful, like Bing, for support and encouragement given when the going was hard. And times in my day were always hard.

The gawping schoolboy of 1947 kept coming back - in the early days as a Festival-goer, then as journalist and broadcaster, before finally joining Frank Dunlop's management team for eight hectic years.

Arts administrators are adept at handling the day-to-day problems that plague Festival organisers - last-minute cancellation by a violin virtuoso; a fit of the sulks from a principal dancer fifteen minutes before curtain up; strike threats from stage crews; even an entire orchestra stranded on the tarmac at Moscow airport in the midst of the plot to oust Gorbachev.

But when the problem involves dealing with bodies and individuals outside the closed community of the arts - as it always does where money is involved - then things are really rough. Tempers get shorter, egos are bruised, and relationships are frequently damaged beyond repair.

The Festival, in my day, expected to raise something over 40 per cent of its revenue at the box office. The rest comes from four principal sources - Edinburgh District Council, the Scottish Arts Council, Lothian Regional Council, and from the business community at large via sponsorship.

While this city of enlightenment still has its men and women of vision, it has also spawned one or two small-minded people of a more parsimonious disposition.

SIR HENRY RAEBURN 1756-1823
The greatest Scottish portraitist, he painted Scott, Hume, Boswell, Christopher North, Lord Melville, Niel Gow, Lord Jeffrey and Lord Cockburn. The Macnab, his best work, fetched £25,400 in 1917.

SUSAN FERRIER 1782-1884
Scotland's Jane Austen.
Wrote *'Marriage'* 1818,
'The Inheritance' 1824
and *'Destiny'* 1831.
One of Scotland's
greatest female novelists.

Such people mistrust the Festival, though they seem to do so for different reasons, according to which side of the political spectrum they favour. Some Conservatives regularly accused the Festival of giving a platform to dangerous undesirables - Marxists, sexual deviants, blasphemers, drug addicts and the like.

And when the city's administration became a Labour one in 1984, things did not alas change. Almost the first public pronouncement by the city's new Labour leadership began with the words: *"The Edinburgh Festival is stuffed-shirt and élitist, and has no relevance to the lives of the ordinary people of this city."*

Threats followed that the council's grant to the Festival would be reviewed and possibly curtailed. But worse was to come.

The plan to construct a full-scale Festival Opera House, reluctantly promised by the outgoing Tory administration after 26 years of procrastination, was abruptly cancelled. The site earmarked for that cancelled Opera House - the infamous "Hole in the Ground" in Castle Terrace - is now occupied by a new office and conference centre, incorporating only a small studio theatre. And that is the first new performance space that Edinburgh has built since well before the Festival began.

Even the new Festival Theatre now under construction in Nicolson Street (which will house opera from 1994) is a converted bingo hall.

Inevitably, Edinburgh is constantly compared to its west-coast neighbour, Glasgow - generally to the latter's advantage. That town, where the city fathers are also Labour, has never grudged putting up new venues for the arts. The Burrell Gallery, the Royal Concert Hall, the Mitchell Theatre are all of very recent construction - as is the Tramway, a truly dramatic performance space created inside the shell of a Victorian tramcar shed.

And of course, Glasgow has had a proper opera house for 20 years.

So is it any wonder that Glasgow was chosen, in preference to Edinburgh, to be Europe's City of Culture in 1990?

But adversity brings its own rewards. And I believe that what makes Edinburgh so very different - and so very superior - to lesser festivals is the ingenuity with which directors and designers constantly overcome the difficulties caused by the dearth of traditional theatres, to stage major productions in the most unlikely venues.

Over the years Festival audiences have enjoyed many magical performances in unusual places - the old Haymarket Ice Rink, the great hall of the Royal Scottish Museum, all the cathedrals and most of the churches of Edinburgh, and of course the Church of Scotland's Assembly Hall.

Every Festival Director is constantly searching for new venues, and I congratulate Brian McMaster and his team for their transformation of the city's Corn Exchange into a theatre to house three of the 1992 Festival's major drama offerings.

Two of the greatest technical achievements I can remember on the

INVESTING IN THE FESTIVAL

For thirty-five years Edinburgh failed to live up to the expectations of its Festival - and the expectations of the millions of people who attended venues that had been starved of desperately needed funding and development.

But in the last few years things have changed. Edinburgh District Council, often working with Lothian and Edinburgh Enterprise Ltd, Lothian Regional Council and private enterprise, has embarked on an ambitious programme of investment.

The aim of this programme is to provide a first class network of arts venues for the 21st century.

Some results can already be seen: there has been a £3.5-million refurbishment of the City Art Centre to create a five floor "supermarket of the arts" which opened in 1992.

The Council is also involved in an extensive refurbishment of the backstage of its King's Theatre, having undertaken a front of house refurbishment at a cost of £1.2 million as recently as 1985.

The Usher Hall is to be extensively upgraded over the next two years and the Assembly Rooms have already benefited from a £2-million programme completed in 1990.

There is a £3.6-million refurbishment of the Royal Lyceum Theatre, of which half has been funded by the council and grants have also been made to the Traverse Theatre in its new home, "The Drum', and to Theatre Workshop.

The new jewel in the Festival's crown, however, will be the 2000-seat Festival Theatre to be completed in time for the 1994 Festival.

The £2.5-million purchase price has been followed by a £11.5-million restoration package that will create one of the country's finest venues and bring back into service a beautiful theatre which latterly had to serve as a bingo hall.

The cost of this whole project is being shared by the council, central government and the private sector (including an important input from LEEL).

LUDOVIC KENNEDY

Born in Edinburgh in 1919.

A journalist for *Newsweek*

***International* and worked on TV.**

Wrote *The Amazing Case of*

***Patrick Meehan* in 1975 which led**

to Paddy Meehan being pardoned.

"official" Festival were both in 1986. One was the creation of an opera house inside a disused town hall at Leith, complete with River Nile running across the stage for a Swedish production of *Aida*.

The same year, technicians transformed Robert Adam's Old Quad at Edinburgh University for an open-air production of Euripides' tragedy *Medea*, performed in Japanese by the Toto Company of Tokyo.

There were to be only three performances, and they were all sell-outs. On the final night, the heavens opened and rain poured down with all the fury of a

THE HISTORY OF THE FESTIVAL

The Edinburgh Festival first took place in August 1947. The Festival was the brainchild of Rudolf Bing, the brilliant Austrian conductor. It had taken him almost two years to put the first Festival together, during which time he laid the foundations for a Festival that would become the biggest and best-known in the world.

Bing courted all the dignitaries in the city to get their support in getting the festival off the ground, and in this regard his knight in shining armour was Harvey Wood, who used all his many contacts in Edinburgh society to gather support.

Bing's brilliant negotiating skills were successful in persuading the Lord Provost and the City Council to support his scheme, and with his festival now off the ground, Bing must have thought it rather appropriate that the very first event of the first Edinburgh Festival was a Songs of Praise held in St Giles Cathedral - it would not be the first time that the director would 'thank God' for the start of an Edinburgh Festival!

The Festival has of course changed very much since 1947. Its first phase was dominated by Bing's long shadow, the second was the domination of Grand Opera until 1978 and the third was the revolution and populism of Drummond and Dunlop.

After Bing came Ian Hunter in 1950, and then Robert Ponsonby in 1955. All three had worked together at Glyndebourne. Bing had been General Manager at the same time as being Director of the Edinburgh Festival. Hunter had worked on the opera staff at Glyndebourne with Ponsonby as his assistant. Bing's influence lasted for more than a decade and little in the structure of the Festival changed until the 60s. The 1950s were to be years of development but essentially only within the pattern which Bing had established.

George Lascelles, the 7th Earl of Harewood, took over in 1961, and his years in charge were arguably the highlight of the Festival's musical years. His concerts were acclaimed as attacking, enthusiastic and brilliant.

MURIEL SPARK OBE

Born 1918. Wrote *The Prime of*

***Miss Jean Brodie* and other**

novels. Jean Brodie was modelled

on Muriel Spark's own teacher at

Gillespies, Miss Christina Kay.

summer storm. Hundreds of ticketless Festival-goers flocked to Old Quad, hoping desperately for returns as any fair-weather members of the audience scurried for cover. They were disappointed: the bulk of the audience sat tight.

The Japanese actors, who insisted that the show must go on whatever the weather, willingly gave an unscheduled extra performance the following night to cope with the demand.

The production - a triumph by the company and director Yukio Ninagawa - went to the National Theatre in London the following year. But not even the National could match the amazing wizardry of the Edinburgh Festival technical crew, who created the huge fiery dragon which swooped down from Edinburgh's night sky, high above the Old College rooftops, to the rescue of Medea.

Our friends on the other Festivals have venue problems as well. The Tattoo, which has thumped and marched its glorious way round the Castle

Esplanade since 1950, keeps hinting strongly that it wants to find another venue, although I hope it doesn't. But I do appreciate the difficulties. It takes about three months to erect the scaffolding and seats, and then another three months to dismantle the whole clamjamfray - all at vast expense, and constant worry, about breaking court injunctions which insist that the work be done in total silence so as not to annoy the neighbours in Ramsay Gardens.

The Jazz Festival, used to rasping out its merry noise in city pubs, has now gone the whole logical hog. For the 1992 Festival the main performance venue

SIR BASIL SPENCE 1907-1969
Architect. Best known for his
brilliant and controversial design
for the new Coventry Cathedral.

He brought great conductors such as Guilini and Boulez to the Festival, with Boulez set to become a great Festival figure. Harewood's successor, Peter Diamand, was the "opera" Director. His and Claudio Abbado's *Carmen* was hailed as outstanding, as was his *Marriage of Figaro* with Sir Geraint Evans and Dietrich Fischer-Dieskau. Drama and theatre were to begin their renaissance at the Festival with Drummond's arrival and it has been he and Dunlop who have shaped today's Edinburgh Festival.

By the time Drummond took over in 1979, the Festival was a great international event, with the Fringe an integral and important part of it. What Drummond did though was to tackle what had been one of the strongest criticisms of the Festival - it may have been international enough but it had never been Scottish enough. He searched for the best and most original of Scottish material and he found it. He had four illustrious years at the helm, culminating in his "Vienna 1890" theme of 1983, before passing that stick of dynamite known as the Director's job to Frank Dunlop.

Dunlop was nothing if not controversial. He will be remembered for many things, but perhaps most of all his conquering *Macbeth*, performed by the Japanese theatre company, Toto. The new emphasis on Scottish literature resulted in MacDiarmid's *A Drunk Man Looks at the Thistle,* Sir David Lyndsay's *Ane Satyre of the Thrie Estaitis* (repeated from earlier years) and Sydney Smith's *The Wallace* in 1985. Dunlop also continued to encourage the expansion of the Festival - not just music and theatre, but now the Book Festival, Film Festival, Jazz Festival and Television Festival - and of course, let's not forget that one evening in the year when it is guaranteed to rain, the Military Tattoo. The Festival grows ever larger and better.

Who knows what the present Director Brian McMaster will bring to the people of Edinburgh and the world of the arts. Whatever he does, the Edinburgh International Festival will continue to be a unique delight, challenging, innovative, controversial, good and bad.

But the important thing is that it will always be Edinburgh's Festival.

was in a brewery. I wholeheartedly approve.

The Book Festival, which also generally manages to house a few Jazzfest gigs, sets itself up in a tented village in Charlotte Square every alternate year. But the real veterans of ingenuity when it comes to creating venues are the Fringe companies.

They will perform anywhere they can get an audience - in a motor-cycle sidecar, in private houses, in scout huts, church halls, up closes, and even on the open street, for not everybody can afford the gilded luxury of the Assembly Rooms (another Robert Adam building).

Most performers on the Fringe are here to enjoy themselves while hoping to be "discovered" and taken on to greater glory in television, or in London's West End. Many are, among them Rowan Atkinson, Rory Bremner, and Fry and Laurie. (By the way, the Fringe always gets the credit for finding the satirists, and

ALEXANDER NASMYTH
1758-1840. Painter.
"Father of the Scottish Landscape".
Also did many pieces of theatrical
scenery for theatres in London
and Glasgow.

mostly it's well-deserved. But the most famous of them all - the Beyond The Fringe team of Peter Cook, Dudley Moore, Alan Bennett and Jonathan Miller - appeared on Robert Ponsonby's official Festival in 1960.)

The most explosive character on the Fringe has been around for a long time, although he keeps threatening to leave in a huff, taking his undoubted talent and energy to Poland. He is, of course, the irrepressible Ricky Demarco, painter, gallery owner, impresario, and non-stop controversialist.

For every Festival as long as I can remember he has staged Fringe plays, events, "happenings" and exhibitions at his own ramshackle galleries in Jeffrey Street and Blackfriars Street. He it was who staged *Macbeth* several years running in the most splendid venue in the history of the Fringe - among the ruins of the priory on Inchcolm Island - conveying audience and actors there nightly in a

Mhairi
MacKenzie Robinson

EDINBURGH FESTIVAL
fringe *

In August 1992, at the height of our Festival, I asked the Director of the Adelaide Fringe, who was visiting Edinburgh for the first time, what surprised him most about the City. I expected him to be gobsmacked with the scale and diversity of the Fringe and the business of the whole city at festival time. This subsequently turned out to be the case, but to him, the real stunner was discovering that Edinburgh's New Town turned out to be Georgian and built in stone. In fact it was 200 years older than he had expected and not a drop of concrete in sight!

Edinburgh is a paradox. Its Old Town is old; its New Town is old. Like Rome it has seven hills, but also sea and as well as being Europe's second largest financial centre, it is also the home of the world's most celebrated and famous arts festivals. In fact Edinburgh is The Festival City and each year hundreds of thousands flock to enjoy its ten major cultural events. It is small in scale and yet as a

European capital, multinational companies have their headquarters within the city. Brewing, publishing and printing, medical research and pharmaceuticals, the seat of the Law and the Church in Scotland are all synonymous with Edinburgh. Sailing, skiing and golf can all be enjoyed on the same day within minutes of each other and to top this, its half-million residents enjoy the best drinking water and standard of lifestyle in the United Kingdom. What I like most about the city are the views. Whichever way you turn, the eye is surprised. The sea is never far from view and walking down the Royal Mile in the heart of the Old Town, it seems only a stone's throw across Holyrood Palace and the Royal Park to Gosford Bay and Aberlady beyond. Looking north over Princes Street from the quiet and secret seclusion of Ramsay Gardens with the colonnaded grandeur of the Royal Scottish Academy and the National Gallery to the right, the Firth of Forth appears to none-too-large boat across the choppy waters of the Firth of Forth.

All this, and much more, he has accomplished in spite of a less than helpful Scottish Arts Council. But the most wounding snub of Ricky's career came in 1991, when he formally applied for the vacant directorship of the official Festival - for which he had actually been shortlisted in 1983 but was pipped on the post by Frank Dunlop. Everyone in the arts community knew that he wasn't going to get the job this time either; indeed I am convinced that Ricky knew it himself.

But you would think that someone of Demarco's stature - truly one of Edinburgh's Men of Vision - would be entitled, if not to an interview before the appointments board, then at least to a warm personal letter from those making the appointment.

Not a bit of it. What Ricky Demarco got, from the board's "search

rise in the distance above and beyond the city, only stopped in its tracks by the Fife villages of Aberdour, Burntisland and the more northern Lomond Hills. People say that you can always tell what the weather is going to do by the glassiness and mirage-like appearance of this stretch of water and if Fife is within touching distance, rain is on the way. From one optical illusion to another, Calton Hill, topped with the Observatory, National Monument and Nelson's Monument, for some reason, has the effect of making any casual walker on its summit appear gigantic. For one's own aggrandisement and uplift, stand between the columns of the National Monument, or 'Edinburgh's Disgrace' as it is affectionately known, on this same hill, and look at the vista along Princes Street at dusk to Corstorphine Hill. The setting sun in the west is breathtaking!

For me, each August, Edinburgh as a city becomes the jewel in the crown of all places to be. It is

Festival time, and for three and a half weeks, it is the time when everyone lets their hair down and indulges in the arts and culture. Edinburgh becomes a city en fete where the rigidity of the normal social rules disappear and the perceived shyness and demureness of its citizens is teased out. It is as acceptable to be silly as it is to go to the theatre four or five times in any one day. In fact it is a must and something which half the population of the city do with the greatest of pleasure. Edinburgh people are culture vultures and the August festivals whet their appetites.

In 1947 final plans were made to stage the first International Festival, as a post-war initiative to re-unite Europe through culture. Unknown to each other or to the official organisers, eight uninvited theatre companies were making their own arrangements to come to Edinburgh. Feeling spurned and excluded from the first Festival Programme, they arrived in

SIR ARTHUR CONAN DOYLE
1859-1930. Studied medicine at
Edinburgh University. Writer and
creator of Sherlock Holmes.

committee" (a mix of city councillors, academics and bankers) was a stereo-typed one-sentence acknowledgement of his job application which "would not be proceeded with".

As I said a moment ago there are some small-minded people in high places. There always will be. But there will always be men and women of vision as well and so the Edinburgh Festival will continue on its glorious way achieving ever greater heights

Councillors - of whatever political persuasion - will continue to keep it short of funds, as will central government via the Arts Council. But the Festival will continue to generate vast revenues for the economy of the city. In 1991 the official Festival cost about £4.2 million, with about a million-and-a-half coming from the box office, the rest from public and business funding. In return Festival visitors

EDINBURGH FESTIVAL
fringe

Edinburgh to make their own mark and add their own artistic style to the schedule of events. They found halls that were not being used by the International Festival, and using skill and imagination, turned empty spaces, into theatres. In essence they found themselves on the "fringe" of the Festival and not in the main pro-gramme of events. These companies attracted audiences, received favourable notices for their shows, and without being invited or guided by an artistic director as to what to perform, had the freedom to stage whatever they liked. By 1958, the Fringe was here to stay but a step towards permanence and continuity was required. An administrative body known as the Festival Fringe Society was formed to offer advice and guid-ance to anyone who wished to take part in future years. Simple and prac-tical aims were drawn up. The Society would publish a complete Programme of all the events not list-ed in the official Festival programme,

it would operate an information office for performers and public alike, and run a club and central box-office from which all groups' tickets could be sold. No artistic selection process or artistic censor-ship would be imposed, leaving that decision to the performers to make up their minds as they saw fit. Some thirty years on and four Administrators later, the same rules apply today.

From *Cymbeline* on Calton Hill, jazz in the park on a summer's after-noon, magic in the morning, fast-talking stand-up late at night to poetry in the courtyard, Shakespeare for breakfast, classical interludes at lunch to ceilidhs after dark, the Fringe offers entertainment and theatre to fill every hour of the day. It is a hot-bed of talent. In 1992, 540 companies from 23 different nations took part in the Fringe. From Malibu to Moscow, Bulawayo, Cologne, Sydney to Dayton, Ohio, this festival had an international gathering of spent an estimated £50 million in the city's shops, restaurants pubs and hotels - according to an official survey carried out for Edinburgh's tourist marketing board.

Further predictions: the Festival will at long last get its opera house the year after next. And it looks as if the Government has been persuaded to fund the much-needed extension to the Royal Museum of Scotland just round the corner.

Thereafter I don't expect either local or national government to fund any new venues in Edinburgh for a further 50 years. Meanwhile Glaswegians will continue to point with pride at their new halls and theatres, and will still be gloating about the triumphs of 1990 well into the next century.

Let them. *Glasgow was chosen to be European Capital of Culture for one year. Edinburgh is the World's Capital of Culture in perpetuity.*

ALLAN RAMSAY 1713-1784
Portrait painter. Travelled on
continent in 1736 and formed a select
Society with David Hume and
Adam Smith.

Allan Ramsay
(Edinburgh Central Library)

artistic talent and inventiveness to celebrate. New plays, both British and world premieres, comedy, dance, folk, classical and world music, children's shows and exhibitions filled every corner and by 5 September, when the final curtain came down, some 624,000 tickets had been sold to people from all over the world, but more especially to people living and working in Edinburgh.

I can think of no better place in which to stage such an event. Amateur and professional, famous and infamous, inside or outside, Edinburgh is transformed by the festivals into the largest stage in the world. It is contained and compact and yet grand and gracious. For all its hills and chilling east wind, it is a place in which to walk. Within the centre, few property developers or urban regenerators have had their evil way with concrete, leaving houses, offices and shops to sit side by side as neatly and comfortably as in

many small villages. Edinburgh is more than the sum of all its parts - it has heart and soul and is as special a place as you are likely to find in any corner of the world.

In the words of Miles Kington, trying to describe Edinburgh is "like trying to describe the buzz of New York, the non-stop activity of India or the stupidity of the English licensing laws. They all have to be experienced. Edinburgh is an illusion which cannot be recreated anywhere else. It is no use trying to tell people about it, only trying to get them to go there."

The Lyceum Theatre. *(City Art Centre, Edinburgh)*

*'Edinburgh
seems like a
Scandinavian
capital. It's very
different from
England and
very refreshing'*

PETER USTINOV

Korean Music and Dance

BESIDE THE SEA

NIGEL TRANTER

Nigel Tranter OBE has been a novelist
and author since 1936. Some of his most
famous novels include *Macgregor's Gathering*,
The Young Montrose and the *Robert the Bruce* trilogy.
He has also written children's novels and
some non-fiction about Scotland.
He was Chairman of the Society of Scottish Authors
from 1966-72, and was
BBC Radio Scotland Man of the Year 1989.

*'As a boy, Granton
beach, harbour and
breakwater was my
playground and
chosen destination
for every Sunday
afternoon'*

The City of the Seven Hills has a preoccupation with salt-water, considering that its centre is only two miles from its coastline on the Firth of Forth.

The reason for the burgh being there at all is undoubtedly because of two necessary features - the upthrusting Castle Rock, for defence and security, and the proximity to the Forth estuary and the North, or Norse Sea, as it used to be called. The very fact that the Forth was long ago known as the Scotwater speaks for itself. Moreover, from any number of places and positions in the city, the blue - admittedly sometimes grey - Forth may be seen and grips and holds the attention, from street-corners and terraces and tenements as well as from the seven hills: Arthur's Seat, Calton, the Castle Rock itself, the Braids and the rest. Few cities can have such widespread vistas and challenging panoramas as has Scotland's capital; and for that, the Firth of Forth, averaging about ten miles in width and reaching nearly sixty in length (all of which can be seen from Edinburgh), can take most of the credit. Small wonder that its citizens, "east windy and west endy", according to the Glasgow folk (prejudiced of course), are apt to be very much aware of the sea and the far prospects.

Personally, I am no exception. Although I was born in Glasgow I was brought to Edinburgh at the age of four and grew up in the city, only leaving it, married, at the age of twenty-eight (in 1938) for the comparable metropolis of Aberlady, sixteen miles down the coast, where I have lived ever since - and which is even more sea-dominated. As a boy, Granton beach, harbour and breakwater was my playground, and chosen destination for every Sunday afternoon walk whatever the season and the weather - although my idea of actual heaven was reserved for Elie, on the other, Fife side of the Forth, for holidays, where my family had a modest summer residence.

Newhaven fisher folk. *The Cavaye collection of Thomas Begbie prints (City Art Centre, Edinburgh)*

The cliffs of Elie are readily seen from many parts of Edinburgh, twenty-odd miles away. That is the sort of preoccupation that the salt-water had and has for the citizenry. They overlook the sea, while being unable to overlook it - if you get my meaning!

We must not forget Leith, of course - the Leithers never allow us to do so! Leith is the port of Edinburgh. It has been since the land and harbour were granted to Holyrood Abbey by its founder, King David the First, in 1128, with the haven actually transferred to the city itself by Robert the Bruce in the year of his death, 1329, as *'ane right of the harbour and mills of Leith, With their appurtenances, to the city of Edinburgh'.* But the good folk of Leith have always made a point of maintaining their own separate identity, as indeed they had a right to do, for it was a separate burgh until amalgamation with the capital, for better or worse, in 1920. There are still rumblings about that.

The Lothian coastline, with Edinburgh in its central position, stretches for fifty miles - from North Berwick town, with its so prominent conical Law and the towering stack of the Bass Rock rising from the waves, on the east, to the West Lothian border with Stirlingshire, at Bo'ness - really Boroughstoneness - in the west. What a challenging, exciting and varied coastline, it is: cliffs, creeks, wide bays, long sandy beaches, fishing villages, small towns and offshore islands, all with their own attractions and stories, some of these of joy and comedy, others grim indeed, for the Scots have never been a people to do things by half, good or bad. Even the name Lothian itself, is storied - for once it was dominated by a very different prominence from Edinburgh's Castle Rock, this being Traprain Law, east from Haddington, the 'capital' of East Lothian, easily seen from the city. Here was the seat of King Loth who gave the counties of East, West and Midlothian their names in the early 6th century. And Loth left his mark on more than the names of

'What a wonderful City Edinburgh is! What alternation of Height and Depth!'

SAMUEL TAYLOR COLERIDGE

these counties - on the forty-miles-away Glasgow itself, indeed, however much the Glaswegians may deplore the fact. For Loth, a pagan, had a daughter Thanea, who was a Christian. Because she refused to marry a pagan princeling chosen for her by her father and was thereafter raped by the rejected Prince Owen, she was condemned to death by her stern father when found to be pregnant, and handed over by him to the tender mercies of Loth's favourite deity, the seagod Manannan. This was arranged by taking her down to the shore of great Aberlady Bay - where my own house nestles at the tide's edge - and cast adrift in a small coracle without a paddle. The tide took poor Thanea out as far as the Isle of May at the mouth of the estuary (again visible from high ground in the city) and there turned, and the coracle carried up-Forth until it grounded at Culross on the Fife shore, just opposite Boroughstoneness where at this time (517 AD), St Serf had a monastery, one of the very few left over after St Ninian's efforts to Christianise the Picts and North

THE WILDLIFE OF EDINBURGH'S COASTLINE

Sudheer Carroll

SOUTH **QUEENSFERRY** is famous for the impressive views of its road and rail bridges, but at the same time the fore-shore west of the rail bridge affords good views of wading birds at low tide. The Common Seal will sometimes venture as far up the Forth estuary as the bridges. At the top of the rise behind the sea-front a strip of mature pine woodland marks the line of a former railway and is home to several species of Tit as well as Grey Squirrel.

Between South Queensferry and Cramond lies the well-wooded Dalmeny Estate; a coastal track provides the walk-er with a countryside route as far as the Cramond ferry. For large parts of the way the track passes through estate plantations and woodland with mature forest trees. One can find Scots Pine, Oak, Sycamore, Lime, Birch and, nearer to Dalmeny house, Horse and Sweet Chestnuts. On one part of the route is an attractive plantation of mixed Beech and Larch carpeted beneath with ferns. The woodlands shelter a rich bird population with Mistle and Song Thrush, Blackbird, Robin, Willow Warbler, Tree-Creeper, Woodpecker,

Wren and many more. Colourful wild flowers can be seen growing in profusion along the wayside: Hedge Woundwort and Red Campion, Ground Ivy and Valerian, Comfrey and Herb Robert can all be found.

There is easy access to sandy beaches strewn with sea-shells, especially Mussel and Cockle. After stormy weather stranded jelly-fish can be found in large numbers. Towards the westward end are areas of sand-dune and one can see the effect of Marram Grass in binding the sand against the prevailing wind. Small rocky headlands provide pools to explore as the tide recedes, with different kinds of green and brown seaweeds, small crabs and other sea-shore creatures.

CRAMOND is a picturesque old village lying at the mouth of the River Almond and is a favourite spot for Mute Swan to congregate at the end of the summer when more than 30 may be seen at one time. A causeway passable at low tide leads out to **CRAMOND ISLAND** and provides a grandstand view of the flocks of wading birds which come there to feed on the extensive

mud-flats. These include such species as Dunlin, Redshank, Golden and Grey Plover and Turnstone, as well as large numbers of Black-Headed and Common Gulls.

An area of old sand-dune is stabilised by Lyme Grass, recognisable by its glaucous blue leaves. Above the high tide mark, the spring-flowering Sweet Cicely, with its anise-scented leaves, lines the promenade. The sea-front extends two miles eastwards by **SILVERKNOWES** to **CRAIGROYSTON** with parkland behind: Pied Wagtail can be seen running across the short mown grass. The sea-wall and path continue another half-mile behind industrial developments to the harbour at **GRANTON.** Although the landward view is not attractive this is a good stretch from which to watch Tern fishing. These swift and elegant birds nest in large colonies on Inchmickery Island not far out in the Forth. The ferry which crosses from Granton harbour to Fife often rewards passengers with the sight of Eider and other sea duck, and of Shag skimming low over the water.

The sea-front embankment at **WARDIE** is currently undergoing environmental improvement. In Victorian times the rocky shore was a fertile hunting ground for geologists who found a great variety of fossil fishes from the Carboniferous Era. **LEITH** docks are situated where Edinburgh's river, the Water of Leith, joins the Forth. Around the old docks and the banks of the lower reaches of the river one can still find exotic wild plants introduced accidentally from ships' cargoes, such as Oriental Rocket and Yellow Bristle Grass.

At the eastern end of the Edinburgh shoreline between **MUSSELBURGH** racecourse and the sea, there is an area of great wildlife interest. This part of the coast has been used as a dump for fly-ash from the nearby Cockenzie power station, creating areas of new land. These are being grassed over and two large fresh-water lagoons have been made: one of these is available for water-sports and a strip of flowering meadow has been established along its western side. Both lagoons provide a welcome resting

place for migrating waterfowl in the colder part of the year.

On the Forth itself many kinds of sea duck inhabit the inshore waters, such as Common and Velvet Scoter, Eider, Scaup, Goldeneye, Long-tailed Duck and Shelduck, whilst a great variety of waders exploit the tidal mud-flats. The new grassland by the sea is being colonised by colourful patches of summer wildflowers: golden Bird's Foot Trefoil, indigo-blue Buglass and lemon yellow Melilot. One may even startle a hare from its resting place in the grass.

Old dune areas have been landscaped with shelter belts of Alder, Aspen, Goat Willow and Rowan, providing homes for many small birds and mammals. An inquisitive stoat may watch the passer-by from the roadside. Grassed-over areas are a favourite foraging ground for small flocks of brightly coloured Oyster Catcher which could, perhaps, become a fitting emblem for the whole of Edinburgh's coastline. It can certainly be seen almost anywhere whenever you choose to walk Edinburgh's shores.

Britons, druidical sun-worshippers. Serf took the girl in, and there her son was born, and christened Kentigern, although Serf called him Mungo (meaning *manikin*). When he grew to man's estate, he, with his mother, travelled westwards to the Clyde estuary on their own monastic and mIssionary endeavours, and at the Molendinar Burn founded his cell, church and settlement, *Glas Ghu* - Glasgow. So, like it or not, the denizens of Scotland's largest community owe their origin to a pair from Lothian. Oddly they call Thanea St Enoch - but then, as any Edinburgh character will tell you, "Glesca keelies canna spell!"

My own predilection for this Lothian coastline is very basic, and I would not wish to live anywhere else. Here I earn my living, on the coast and seaboard itself, for I write as I walk, have done ever since my war-years, when the only privacy I could achieve for producing novels in the army was to get out and away from my fellows and write as it were "on the hoof". Some seventy-odd novels (odd in more ways than that) have been written in my daily walking round Aberlady Bay and Gullane Point and Bay and on past St Patrick's Chapel - he was from our Scotland, you know, before becoming patron-saint of Ireland - to Freshwater Haven and Muirfield Bay, where the Honourable Company of Edinburgh Golfers have their famous Open Championship links; and still further, when I am feeling energetic, to where I can see the string of islands, Eyebroughty, Fidra, the Lamb, Craigleith, the soaring Bass and eventually far-away May itself on the blue horizon, a sight to see and to stimulate.

Aberlady Bay, now a nature reserve, is extraordinary in itself, unique on the Forth estuary in that it is over one thousand acres. It dries out at low-water and then presents a great plain fringed with the green tidelands, with a sand-bar at the mouth over two miles long, and yet fills up fully indeed at high-water so that you could sail a boat almost to my gate. This the haunt of sea-birds and wildfowl inumerable, the wild geese in their thousands flighting, the ducks quacking, the eiders crooning and the curlews wheepling. Enough to come between a man and his scribbling, no?

'The abomination of Granton Pier, with its tram-roads, brickwork and quarry'

LORD COCKBURN

Nearer the city are lesser bays and beaches but no less notable places and features: Gosford and Seton - historic indeed, for to Seton Mary Queen of Scots came after the murder of her second husband, Darnley, with her third husband-to-be, Bothwell, and there *"won an archery contest against the Lord Seton her most faithful adherent, and the Earl of Huntly in lieu of mourning"*, and here her son James VI and I paused on his way south to take over Elizabeth's throne in 1603 and found the United Kingdom. The ancient burgh of Cockenzie and Port Seton is nearby, refusing to be dominated by its enormous modern powerstation, however much this spoils the view from Edinburgh; and then there is Prestonpans, or Salt Preston, where not only salt was made from sea-water, essential for Scotland's

The Forth Rail Bridge under construction, 1891

important trade in salt-fish and meat, but where pottery which has become famous and scarce was manufactured. Moreover it is where Bonnie Prince Charlie won his great victory in 1745, and where he should have turned back to become King of Scots instead of pressing on to defeat at Derby and afterwards lonely exile in France.

Musselburgh, that stalwart town, sits at the mouth of the River Esk - indeed it has the alternative name of Inveresk, where the Romans established a centre - close now to the Edinburgh boundary, but which, unlike Leith, has managed to retain its independence;

"Musselburgh was a burgh when Edinburgh was nane, And Musselburgh will be a burgh when Edinburgh's gane." The Honest Toun, as it calls itself still, was given that name by Bruce's nephew, Moray, Regent for his infant son David II, who died here - *honest* in this case meaning reliable, faithful to the cause.

Portobello and Joppa, to the west, may sound strange names for suburbs of Edinburgh, but until 1762 the area was called Figgate Whins, a barren stretch of moor, gorse and sand. Then a retired sailor built a cottage here, by the Figgate Burn, and named it Portobello, after the town of that name in Panama, at the siege of which he had been present. Three years later a valuable bed of clay

*'The banks
of the river were
tangled brakes
of bramble
and hawthorn.
The water abounded
with different species
of minnow, and
in some parts with
fine trout'*

**CUMBERLAND
HILL**

Harry Lauder

was found here leading to development of a pottery and brack-making. Thus the community grew. Here Walter Scott began his *Lay of the Last Minstrel*; the famous Hugh Miller, geologist and author, shot himself in 1856; and Harry Lauder was born in 1870.

The locally-renowned Fishwives' Causeway started here, leading from the shoreline to the city; and along this the fishermen's women used to trudge daily with their great basket-creels on their backs, the supporting straps actually round their foreheads, cheerfully, chanting their own overture:

'Wha'll buy my caller herrin', bonny fish and halesome farin',
Wha'll buy my caller herrin' new drawn frae the Firth?'

I can just remember these sturdy ladies' solid build, necessarily so, and their thick blue serge skirts.

Leith Links, coming next, is alleged to be the original location for the game of golf, not as is usually claimed, St Andrews, home of the Royal and Ancient course. Here Kings of Scots *"played at the golf"*, from James III's time, and Charles I was actually golfing here when informed of the outbreak of rebellion in Ireland in 1641.

'The glorious Forth, all silent, serene, sublime'

PROF. JOHN WILSON

Beyond Leith is Newhaven, now largely a pleasure-boat anchorage with attractive old-fashioned buildings, but originally called Our Lady's Port of Grace. Here was built, in 1511, James IV's idea of starting a Scots navy, *"ane varie monstrous great schip called the Michel"*, requiring so much fine timber that *"she waisted all the woodes in Fyfe except Falkland Wood, besides the timber that came out of Norway"*. Leith superseded Newhaven and it sank to being merely a fishing-village, although in 1884 it is recorded as having thirty-three first-class and one hundred and seventy second-class boats, manned by four hundred and twenty-eight fishermen and boys.

Granton thereafter, already mentioned, leads on along the coast by Royston, now backed by the large housing concourse of Pilton, presently to Cramond, a delightful community at the mouth of the River Almond - the name derived from Caer Almond, the Celtic and then Roman fortlet. Inland from here a little way, at

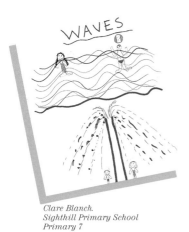

Clare Blanch.
Sighthill Primary School
Primary 7

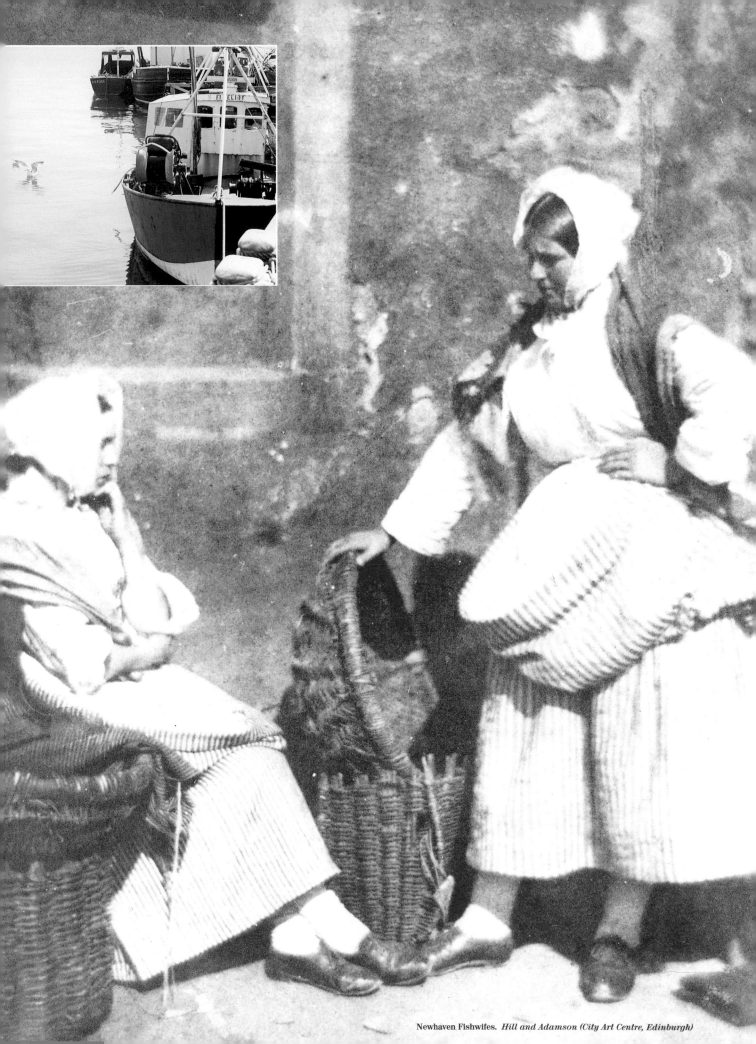

Newhaven Fishwifes. *Hill and Adamson (City Art Centre, Edinburgh)*

Marchfield, was bred by William Sharpe a mare named Martha Lynn, from which all the best racing blood in England is asserted to be descended. Cramond Tower, recently restored to be a lived-in house from ruin, was the 15th-century residence of the Bishops of Dunkeld. Offshore is Cramond Island, where many an adventurous youngster has been marooned, for it is reachable on foot at low-water - but the tide can turn swiftly and cut it off!

Other islands in the Forth's mid section, easily seen from Edinburgh, are Inchkeith, Inchcolm and Inchmickery. Inchkeith is famous for a notable experiment. The aforementioned and enterprising James IV wondered what was the *natural tongue of mankind*", believing it, allegedly, to be Gaelic. He marooned a dumb woman on the island, with two infants, and left them there, to discover what language the children would eventually speak; he claimed, in time, that *"they spak very guid Hebrew"*. But in fact, all three starved to death during a period of storms with no food reaching them.

Inchcolm, called after St Columba as the hermitage of one of that great character's missionaries, was then called Aemonia - figuring as such in Shakespeare's *Macbeth*. In 1123, King Alexander I was crossing the Forth when a storm overturned his boat and he was stranded on this island, where he had to remain, with the hermit, living on shellfish, for three days, until signals to the Fife shore brought rescue. He founded the Augustinian abbey thereon, in honour of Columba, in gratitude, and it is still a place of pilgrimage for modern visitors.

Not far between these two islands on the Fife side, was the scene of another royal mishap, with a less happy ending - Kinghorn. Here, in 1286, Alexander III was hastening from Edinburgh on a wild March night, to his lovely new wife's house, against all advice. In the windy dark his horse fell over the Kinghorn head-land's cliff. He was killed - thus leaving no male heir and precipitating the Wars of Independence, Wallace, Bruce and the rest in that mighty saga. Poor Yolande the Queen was kept under care for nine months to see if she produced the desired heir; and when she did not, she was packed off back to her native Dreux, in France.

Dredger, Granton Harbour. *The Cavaye collection of Thomas Begbie prints (City Art Centre, Edinburgh)*

*'The Water
of Leith
where all
the ladies
clean their
teeth'*

WILLIAM McGONAGALL

And beyond that unhappy place are the two great bridges over the Forth, rail and road, at Queensferry, North and South. These get their names from the ferry established here by Margaret, Queen and Saint, in the eleventh century, at the narrows of Forth, to carry pilgrims across to visit the shrine she had established at Dunfermline, where was her husband, Malcolm Canmore's palace - the first stone abbey built in Scotland. They remained ferry-terminals until 1964, by which time unfortunately the traffic for crossing had outgrown the capacity of the boats involved, and mile-long queues developed daily on either side of the water, impatience rampant. I myself suffered much frustration, for at this time my wife and I were constantly travelling all over Scotland for two series of books I was writing and I was no more patient than the rest. Greatly daring, I set up and chaired the National Forth Road Bridge Committee, to agitate and fight for the building of the so-necessary link - at times an infuriating struggle. The challenge was finally met, and the bridge built - it opened in 1964. The view of the two 600-feet of high supporting pillars, readily seen from the city and from far beyond, has some special significance for this writer - even though I was not invited to the Queen's opening thereof, having trampled on too many official toes in the process!

Round the coastline beyond this is out-of-sight from Edinburgh - and anyway enough is enough! Far away, the Ochil Hills draw the eye, and then, eventually, the jagged blue outline of the Highland mountains, from Ben Ledi to Ben Lomond. One looks and looks and wonders . . .

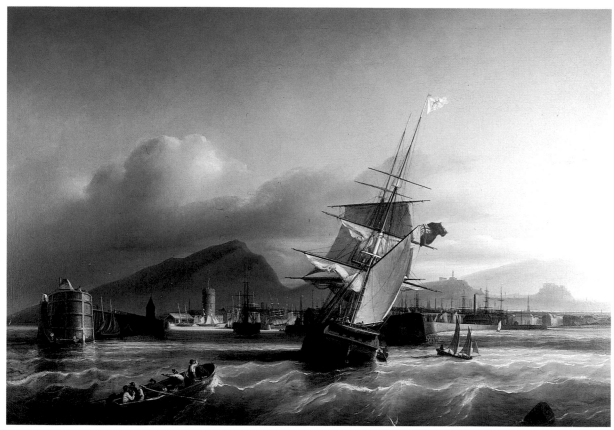

The Port of Leith. *Paul Jean Clays (City Art Centre, Edinburgh)*

EARNING A LIVING

GEORGE KEREVAN

George Kerevan is a District Councillor,
Convenor of the City of Edinburgh District Council
Economic Development Committee
and a senior lecturer
in economics at Napier University.

'...Edinburgh and the great city economies are not merely trading posts: they are the engines of European growth'

The French have a word for it. They differentiate between *grandes villes* and *villes provinciales* - "great cities" and "provincial cities"- *Edimbourg* is a grande ville: after all no other Scottish town has a French translation.

To use a biological analogy, a great city is an economic synapse in the European brain. It is a historic entity that arose out of serving European economic and cultural needs. Provincial cities, on the other hand, are literally cities which grew economically and politically out of their surrounding hinterland and which depend on that hinterland for their continued existence. A *grande ville* is not necessarily large. Venice is a mere 65,000 in population. Edinburgh 420,000. A *ville provinciale* need not be small or parochial; witness Birmingham or Lyons.

Edinburgh is Edinburgh because of the role it has always played historically in Europe not because of its links to its hinterland, which are uniquely few apart from using the neighbouring area as a labour pool. Edinburgh, its port of Leith today Scotland's busiest commercial harbour, is the historic western-most link in the great Baltic/North Sea highway which for centuries has been the main North European trade artery balancing the Mediterranean to the south. From St Petersburg, Stockholm, Rostov or Gdansk westwards to Leith, then south to the Low Countries and France, Europe's commerce and culture has flowed through an Edinburgh entrepot.

But Edinburgh and the great city economies are not merely trading posts; they are the engines of European growth. Barcelona's mayor Pasqual Maragall (who spent his post-Olympic holiday in Edinburgh) explains it this way. In the United States, New York apart, development came by westwards geographical conquest and migration, ultimately via railroad arteries, so that towns were merely railhalts along the pipeline from the economically dominant eastern seaboard. European development experience is different. A settled patchwork of urban centres in Europe interacted with one another from the early Middle Ages, swapping manufactures and ideas across Europe as a whole.

Royal Institution, Castle Princes Street. *J. D. Swarbreck (City Art Centre, Edinburgh)*

This urban network, of which Edinburgh was and is a key part, is the once and future motor of European development. Some west coast towns of Britain, like Liverpool, mushroomed in the nineteenth century as conduits for purely British links with the Empire. But as the importance of these temporary relationships declined in the late twentieth century, the West coast towns shrank while the archetypal Eurocities have entered a new lease of life with the advent of the Single Market and the dramatic fall of the Berlin Wall.

EDINBURGH'S CHANGING ECONOMY

The vital test of a great city is its ability to constantly reinvent its economic rationale. Edinburgh has successfully confronted this dilemma several times.

Edinburgh began to flourish first as a Norman frontier garrison town in the twelfth century, drawing on the pan-European spread of Norman medieval civilisation. Next Edinburgh turned itself into Scotland's capital during the era of Franco-English competition, making excellent use of the times when Scotland was essentially a French colony. Shorn of a Scottish Parliament after 1707, Edinburgh turned to intellectual production in the eighteenth-century Enlightenment, and marshalled its limited capital through the invention of a dynamic banking system to service the building of the New Town (an early version of Canary Wharf with better architecture).

In the nineteeth century, imperial wealth turned Edinburgh into a bastion of the professional middle classes. The arrival of the railways made her for the first time both the centre of a new communications network and a tourist gateway to the North. These developments were symbolised by the Forth (Rail) Bridge, for its time a *tour de force* of European structural engineering and arguably Europe's first piece of modernist architecture (thus roundly hated by the English romantics).

'The New Town arose, growing from day to day, until Edinburgh became one of the most handsome and picturesque cities in Europe'

JAMES NASMYTH

Edinburgh entered the twentieth century with its economy clustered around retail banking, brewing, publishing, shipbuilding and railhead activities. The workforce was swelled by immigration from Ireland, Italy and, via the Baltic, the nationalities of the Russian Empire, giving turn-of-the-century Edinburgh a very cosmopolitan flavour. The heavy commercial and consumer orientation of the economy allowed Edinburgh to ride out the mid-century depression. Banks turned to investing in government bonds and Edinburgh's neglected beaches at Portobello became a major tourist attraction for the Scottish working classes in the era before cheap package holidays to Spain. The magnificent Art Deco edifice of St Andrew's House, opened in 1939, ushered in a new expansion of government administration activity, today accounting for 20,000 Edinburgh jobs.

'Under no circumstances will I ever again be a candidate for Edinburgh'

THOMAS BABINGTON MACAULAY

1947 saw the invention of the Edinburgh Festival and the start of an international tourist market, a bold move made possible only by drawing on the city's belief in itself as a European capital. The wartime arrival of bomb-sight manufacturer Ferranti began the turn to science-based industries. But these promising developments were cut short by the disastrous invention of Scottish New Towns and public subsidy for firms to move out to them from Edinburgh. The sixties saw local industry suffocated.

In the early seventies Edinburgh fumbled, through civic inertia, its chance to attract North Sea oil industry. For a time it looked as if local banking would be absorbed by the City of London. Even Edinburgh's vigorous tourist trade showed a stagnant market share in the seventies when faced with foreign competition. The nadir came in 1979 when the Scots voted by a majority to set up a Parliament in Edinburgh but Westminster shelved the project, leading to a collapse of city confidence.

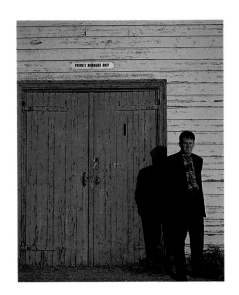

In retrospect, Edinburgh's dormant period in the early post-war decades is explained by its isolation from its natural European roots caused by British rejection of EC membership, the Cold War and ruthless centralisation in London. But those very roots had fashioned for Edinburgh tremendous economic reserves of middle-class ingenuity, financial capital and glorious architectural heritage. In 1984, Edinburgh elected a new city administration headed by fresh young professionals committed to Edinburgh regaining its place as a European capital. And a new generation of business leaders in the Chamber of Commerce published a bold civic plan entitled "Edinburgh's Capital". Slowly, sometimes painfully, Edinburgh reinvented itself in the late 1980s boom.

The City Council invited a series of internationally renowned architects to masterplan the next phase of the city's reconstruction. Sprawling suburbs were contained within a new outer-city bypass and American architect Richard Meier,

famous for the Getty Museum, was put to work on the 180-acre Edinburgh Park at the city's western port. This new urban-dense gateway to Edinburgh will be Britain's largest and most modern business and technology park. Terry Farrell is building a new 1,200-seat conference centre. Two new theatres (including the long sought opera house), two new art galleries and a new museum complex have opened or are under construction. A third university has been created. British Telecom responded to the growth of the financial sector by investing in what it claims is now the most advanced fibre-optic telephone system in Europe. And numerous companies including Dawson International (the world's largest textile multinational) located their head offices in the city.

Today the Edinburgh economy depends not on processing local raw materials for a local market, but in transforming the brainpower of its citizens into services bought by foreigners. Out of 240,000 employed workers, 80,000 work in sectors involving the production and distribution of information related products.

EDINBURGH

The city's economy is now highly diversified with a strong international presence in finance, high technology and tourism.

Germany is the city's largest foreign export customer. Each year Edinburgh's festivals bring 1.3 million visitors into town, three times the local population. Tourism employs over 12,000 people directly in Edinburgh and contributes over £300 million each year to the local economy. In the cultural industries sector, the old mainstay of publishing has given way to some fifteen film and video companies and the largest concentration of graphic design outside of London.

As proof of this newfound economic vitality, at the beginning of 1992 (in the depth of a major economic recession) Edinburgh actually began construction of its equivalent of La Defense business district in Paris, including a major new road entrance into the city and the capital's largest shopping centre.

SCIENCE CITY

The most palpable example of these changes is the economic concentration on science rather than art. In the 1980s the city administrations of Glasgow and Edinburgh pursued diametrically opposite regeneration strategies. Glasgow opted for a "post industrial" concentration on culture. Arts-rich Edinburgh proclaimed itself, perhaps a trifle grandiosely, Science City, and placed emphasis on promoting high technology research and production. This strategy was calculated on the premise that a continuing stake in new technology was necessary to generate the wealth on which service and cultural jobs ultimately depend.

Symbolising the Edinburgh approach was the launch of the world's first annual Science Festival in 1989. This Easter-time festival now attracts 200,000 visitors each year plus world-famous scientists such as Steven Jay Gould, environmentalists such as Jane Goodall, and astronauts such as Allan Shephard, the only man to play golf at both Muirfield and on the moon!

Behind the symbol of the Science Festival lies an imposing high technology research and manufacturing base. Over a quarter of the "value added"

created in the greater Edinburgh economy comes from computer and electronic engineering. The area is Europe's largest producer of silicon chips and hosts the largest concentration of research into artificial intelligence anywhere outside the USA. Output is highly diversified and includes telecommunications, opto-electronics, instrumentation, biotechnology and pharmaceuticals. Electronic engineering is now the city's largest manufacturing industry providing some ten thousand jobs with GEC-Ferranti, Hewlett Packard and Racal-Mesl. Ethicon, a subsidiary of Johnson and Johnson, is Europe's largest producer of surgical sutures. And when the world watched the Olympic Games on television, it did so via satellites lofted into orbit using guidance systems made in Edinburgh.

Edinburgh's claim to a high-tech future rests on the fact that it has already assembled all the vital ingredients that gave Silicon Valley in California a critical mass for a self-sustaining technological growth. These ingredients include:

• World-class basic research facilities: artificial intelligence and medicine at Edinburgh University, fibre optics and petroleum sciences at Heriot-Watt, flexible manufacturing technologies at Napier; these feeding skilled labour and inventions to. . .

• Major international players in high technology manufacturing, e.g. GEC-Ferranti and Hewlett Packard; these spinning off. . .

• Local start up companies pioneering new technologies e.g. Office Work Stations and Spider Systems; but these also need. . .

• Local venture capital potentially arising from Edinburgh being one of Europe's major concentrations of equity funds; plus the added advantage of. . .

• The social, cultural and educational amenities of Edinburgh necessary to attract and hold skilled labour.

But there remains serious structural weakness in Edinburgh's high-tech economy. Firstly, we have a critical lack of civilian applied industrial research to ensure the local economy keeps abreast with the breakneck speed of technological change. This is being addressed by the proposed creation of the Edinburgh Technopole based on the Sophia-Antipolis centre outside Nice which houses IBM's European research HQ. The Edinburgh Technopole, at Edinburgh University's Bush Estate to the south of the city, is being prepared for inward investing Japanese research companies. The Technopole will require a considerable infrastructural investment if it is to succeed.

Secondly, Edinburgh is over reliant on defence contracts. There are some 14 defence contractors in the greater Edinburgh economy employing around 8,000 workers, with over 60% being highly skilled, and a further 10,000 indirectly employed. Forecasts suggest that job losses may reach 13-21% by the end of 1994 as a result of post-Cold War defence cuts. Most threatened is GEC-Ferranti whose Edinburgh plants are the prime contractor for the radar of the European Fighter Aircraft. The local authorities and the Scottish Enterprise Agency are currently hard at work with local defence contractors on a major effort to diversify manufacturing into civilian markets.

ZURICH BY THE FORTH

After its high technology, Edinburgh's best kept secret is the sheer size and international influence of its financial sector. Like Basle or Zurich, Edinburgh's standing comes from discretely investing and managing other people's money. Standard Life, the largest mutual life assurance company in Europe, has its headquarters in Edinburgh.

Starting with the foundation of the Bank of Scotland in 1695 and the Royal Bank in 1727, which still retain their head offices in Edinburgh, the city's financial community has grown to the point where it employs over 20,000 people. Another 20,000 work in various business services such as accountancy and law which directly support the financial sector. Over the 1980s, the number of financial and related companies in Edinburgh doubled to some 1,600. With Edinburgh as the centre, the Scottish financial institutions employ 10% of the Scottish labour force-nine times as much as in heavy industry which used to be the core of the Scottish economy. They generate 15% of Scottish Gross Domestic Product - twice the EC average.

How much truth is there in the oft quoted assertion that Edinburgh is the "second largest financial centre of Europe after London"? There is of course a degree of exaggeration here; which is unfortunate because Edinburgh's powerful financial position does not depend on aping equity and exchange markets like London or Frankfurt.

A city's financial muscle can be gauged by measuring just how much equity funds its moneymen are looking after compared to other cities. Compiling such league tables requires heroic assumptions regarding exchange rates, gyrating stock market valuations, and just how one defines "financial centre" geographically.

With such provisos in mind, it is probably true to say that the funds operating out of Edinburgh and the central belt of Scotland manage sums greater than in any other European Community cities other than London and possibly Dusseldorf. But to keep the record straight, if you include Geneva or Zurich in the picture, each with three times the Edinburgh equity funds base, then Edinburgh slips down the league table. Nevertheless, it is clear that when it comes to deciding

**Lothian and
Edinburgh
Enterprise
Limited**

Sir Charles Fraser
KCVO, WS, DL, Dr.hc.
Chairman

A MESSAGE FROM
SIR CHARLES FRASER

CHAIRMAN OF LEEL

I was born in the Lothians: all my working life has been spent here. This is where I belong and although I have had the good fortune to travel widely, and am fascinated by things foreign, the real interests to which I instinctively return are definitely Scottish.

Lothian place names are redolent of history: Lamerlaw and Caerketon, Pinkie and Prestonpans. Statues of the great adorn our streets - the streets where Simpson lived and Bell was born, to name but two.

A feel for a place and its history is, however, not enough. We must also have a vision of the future. Those that I admire most are men of vision - Dr Willy Robertson of the Scottish Council for Development and Industry, Sir Jamie Stormonth Darling of the National Trust for Scotland, and Dr Morton Boyd of the Nature Conservancy Council. They are three of the great post war visionaries.

We in LEEL share that vision and boldness. We strive after the same high levels of quality and excellence.

Edinburgh and the Lothians are uniquely placed to contribute to wealth and job creation in Scotland. In the faster-growing industries such as tourism, financial services and software we are already forging ahead.

The strength of research and education in our universities and colleges is second to none and we are fortunate indeed in our living and working environment.

LEEL must nurture and build on these strengths in partnership with the private sector, the local authorities and Scottish Enterprise. That is the way we can fulfil a vision of a community thriving amongst great opportunities, and strengthened by training and education.

It is thrilling to be part of a company with such a vision. We have all received a great deal from the city and country of our birth. We can help to repay that debt by making the vision a reality.

Charles J Fraser

Apex House, 99 Haymarket Terrace, Edinburgh EH12 5HD Tel. 031-313 4000 Fax. 031-313 4231

Lothian and Edinburgh Enterprise Limited. Registered in Scotland No 122701 Registered Office, 12 Hope Street, Edinburgh EH2 4DD
Directors: Sir Charles A Fraser (Chairman), D Kinloch Anderson, Dr D Bonnar, K J Geddes, G Korevaar, Prof A G J MacFarlane, F Mackenzie, R M Maiden,
Dr I P Sword, E M Walker, R S Watt, F J Kelly

EDINBURGH'S TOP TEN EMPLOYERS OF PEOPLE

LOTHIAN REGIONAL COUNCIL
Local Authority

GEC FERRANTI DEFENCE SYSTEMS LTD
Defence/Electronics

LOTHIAN HEALTH BOARD
Health Care

SCOTTISH & NEWCASTLE BREWERIES
Brewing/Leisure

SCOTTISH OFFICE
Central Government

ROYAL BANK OF SCOTLAND
Banking

UNIVERSITY OF EDINBURGH
Higher Education

STANDARD LIFE ASSURANCE
Life Assurance

EDINBURGH DISTRICT COUNCIL
Local Authority

BANK OF SCOTLAND
Banking

LEEL IN ACTION

where and how Europe's footloose capital is to be invested, the men and women operating around Edinburgh's Charlotte Square have more influence behind the scenes than their equivalents in Barcelona, Milan, Munich or even Paris.

Edinburgh's strength in fund management is historical: the Scots invented financial trusts as a way of professionally managing and risk spreading the investment of the profits from the great nineteenth-century capital goods industries. But this early start has been capitalised on by exploiting three competitive advantages.

Firstly, Edinburgh's financial sector is a classic example of what American management guru Michael Porter would define as the benefits of an integrated network of quality subcontractors. The Edinburgh financial sector is highly diversified. It has major domestic and foreign retail banks, assurance companies, fund managers, merchant banks, and specialised support in company law, accounting, consultancy, public relations and design. Few cities in Europe can match this range. Further, Edinburgh benefits from the quality resulting from competition within this network.

Secondly, Edinburgh's long-standing international links, reinforced by the personal contacts arising from the diaspora of Scots financial managers around the world, provide both advanced information from the world's equity markets and easy entry to the world's industrial companies.

Thirdly, like Switzerland and patently unlike London, canny Scots conservatism and the intimacy of peer group pressure in Edinburgh mean the city

The importance of tourism to the Lothians is such that it employs over 12,000 people in Edinburgh alone and contributes £300 million to the local economy each year. It is hardly surprising, therefore, that it is one of LEEL's priority target sectors.

As part of its drive to strengthen the region's attractiveness in the face of steadily increasing competition, LEEL is playing a leading role in a number of major developments.

These include the £15 million Younger Universe, a unique world-class environmental visitor attraction housed in an innovative new building at the foot of Edinburgh's historic Royal Mile. Entitled "The Dynamic Earth", the exhibition, due to open in 1995, will use state of the art technology to tell how the earth was created, how it works and mankind's role in protecting its future.

Already under construction is the Edinburgh Festival Theatre, a new 2,000-seat opera house which will give the city for the first time the capability to stage operatic events worthy of its reputation as an international centre of the arts.

To capitalise upon the huge potential provided by the business tourist market, the Edinburgh International Conference Centre is being built at a cost of £36 million. With a capacity to accommodate 1,200 delegates in its main auditorium it is designed to turn the city into one of Europe's premier conference venues and will generate £14 million has escaped both the unjustified over expansion into market-making that followed international financial deregulation and the resulting insider-trading scandals. Edinburgh's financial goldfish bowl reduces the possibility of corruption or stupidity.

Nevertheless, there are problems on the horizon for the Edinburgh financial sector with the advent of the liberalisation of European capital markets. To date, the main equity markets in which Edinburgh fund managers have operated have been in the US and Japan. They are relatively less experienced in operating in the European Community itself. Edinburgh's assurance companies are mutual funds which are therefore protected from predatory take-over though at the price of restricting their equity base. Their UK markets could come under threat from the giant French and German insurers.

WHAT ARE THE INGREDIENTS OF EDINBURGH'S ECONOMIC VITALITY?

An examination of Edinburgh's high technology and financial sectors on the eve of the completion of the Single Market reveals a common thread: can they take successful advantage of a bigger market or will they lose out to European competition? To answer this question properly we have to assess the vitality and capacity for change of the Edinburgh business class.

The powerful personal networks of the Edinburgh bourgeoisie, educated together in Scottish public schools and universities, socially bonded by gentlemen's

---

of revenue each year.

The improvement of Lothian's property and environment, while important for its own sake, is also undertaken by LEEL with a view to how it can make a contribution towards economic development. Thus in its first year, LEEL created more than 125,000 sq ft of top quality business space and cleared some 340 acres of derelict land, bringing it back into commercial use.

In Edinburgh it is involved in the largest city centre development in Scotland - the provision of nearly one million sq ft of prestige office accommodation to cater for the modern requirements of the financial services sector on a nine-acre site with the international conference centre at its heart.

At the Bush Estate in Midlothian, infrastructure work has begun to create the Edinburgh Technopole, Britain's first science city. This £100 million development in partnership with the University of Edinburgh is designed to create up to 5,000 jobs by attracting international research and development organisations to its campus, with manufacturing taking place on a network of related sites.

In terms of high-technology inward investment, West Lothian has Scotland's largest concentration of companies. To ensure a continuing supply of land for this purpose, LEEL has purchased a 75-acre site adjacent to the M8 and the 300 acres on which the former Bangour Hospital was situated.

KEY EMPLOYMENT SECTORS
TOTAL EMPLOYMENT IN EDINBURGH

		1981	1989	%CHANGE
34	Electrical + Electronics Engineering	8225	10191	+23.9%
41/42	Food + Drink	14819	8732	—41.1%
47	Paper, Printing+ Publishing	6302	4251	—32.5%
50	Construction	13003	13459	+3.5%
61	Wholesale Distribution	8245	8164	—1.0%
64/65	Retail Distribution	22376	23091	+18.4
66	Hotel + Catering	11575	13701	+18.4%
79	Post + Telecommunications	6400	3167	—50.5%
81	Banking + Finance	8074	11394	+41.1%
82	Insurance	5560	9942	+78.8%
83	Business Services	11726	20685	+76.4%
85	Dealing in Real Estate	1456	1934	+32.8%
91	Public Administration	20687	19852	—4.0%
93	Education	22651	22028	—2.8%
94	Research + Development	1508	1853	+22.9%
95	Medical + Health Services	18608	18938	+1.8%
96	Other Services to the General Public	11989	11611	—3.2%
97	Recreational + Cultural Services	5470	5492	+0.4%

Source: Census of Employment

SOCIO-ECONOMIC PROFILE

	EDINBURGH	GB
A	4.6%	4.5%
B	16.7%	18.8%
C1	20.0%	9.1%
C2	15.1%	26.2%
D	10.8%	12.2%
E	5.6%	4.1%

Source: Census of Populaton 1981

AGE PROFILE OF
EDINBURGH'S POPULATION (1990)

0-4	26500
5-15	47945
16-24	62693
25-44	132345
45-64	91697
65-74	39210
74+	34132
	434522

Source: General Register Office (Scotland)

AVERAGE GROSS
WEEKLY EARNINGS (£)
LOTHIAN REGION

FULL TIME MALE	MANUAL	216.5
	NON MANUAL	322.6
	OVERALL	274.3
FULL TIME FEMALE	MANUAL	143.1
	NON MANUAL	207.7
	OVERALL	197.4

Source: New Earnings Survey 1990

clubs such as the Edinburgh New Club or lingering medieval fraternities such as the High Constables, have endowed the city with a unique business class. Its solidarity has guaranteed the survival for example of the Royal Bank from the Hong Kong and Shanghai Bank in 1981 or of the brewer Scottish & Newcastle from the Australian Elders IXL group. Its stability has allowed its financiers to take a longer view of investments than the fickle City of London and thus created a business culture that has attracted funds from abroad out of all proportion to the city's size or geography. Above all, for good or ill, Edinburgh's history and physical beauty have bred in its middle classes a profound air of superiority and confidence when facing the rest of the world.

These are the attributes of a patrician class excelling in holding its ground and pursuing its own interests in spite of all comers. But are these the attributes necessary to deal with rapid economic and political change? Bill Ross, Chief Executive of the EDI property company, and one of Edinburgh's perceptive business minds, says of the city's business community that it is characterised by *"traders"* rather than *"deal makers"* and that Edinburgh needs more of the latter. Traders, in his parlance, are very good at minding the shop but not at changing the rules of the game. Hence the Edinburgh financial sector escaped the daftness of post-Big Bang London. But maybe minding the shop is not enough in today's Europe.

LEEL ON TRAINING

LEEL believes firmly that the Lothian's most important resource is its people.

It has set its sights on ensuring that in the years ahead the region has a workforce which is fully equipped to take advantage of the employment opportunities which are presented.

Its policy is to develop training of quality and relevance, whether that be for school-leavers, the adult unemployed or those with jobs who need to learn new skills.

In its first year it invested £17 million in training. Nearly 5,000 young people began some form of skills improvement - and 70 percent of them are now in jobs.

Over 5,000 unemployed adults also benefited from a range of training programmes, the majority linked to the attainment of recognised vocational qualifications.

For those in work, at every level, LEEL has introduced programmes designed to protect their jobs and develop their careers, for example through the Springboard initiative. This helps employers in small to medium-sized companies identify women with management potential and provides personal development programmes for them.

On a wider level, LEEL actively encourages companies to participate in the national Investors in People scheme, which requires them to make a public commitment to invest in quality training linked to the achievement of their business objectives. Those who join have to submit to a rigorous independent assessment by an expert panel, a process which LEEL itself is undergoing.

To help combat a rate of new business start-up which has historically lagged behind the Scottish average, LEEL has introduced a number of initiatives such as LEEP, the Lothian and Edinburgh Enterprise Programme.

This provides business skills training, counselling by experienced professionals, business planning support and financial assistance.

In 1991/92 a total of 531 new businesses were created in this way and LEEL also funded more than 1,400 training days and 100 seminars to give new business owners added support.

It is also devoting its resources to stimulating the growth of existing companies in identified target sectors through a variety of specialist training and management development programmes.

Some 700 small companies have received specialist help with management accounting and marketing, while others were assisted in coping with rapid changes in their marketplace.

With the co-operation of major manufacturers a supplier development initiative has provided small to medium-sized companies with the opportunity to compete for sub-contract work. Others have been helped in their progress towards BS5750 accreditation or the implementation of Total Quality Management programmes.

GETTING UNDER WAY IN BUSINESS

UNEMPLOYMENT IN EDINBURGH AND LOTHIAN EDINBURGH TTWA

	Male No.	Rate	Female No.	Total Rate	No.	Rate
1981	18053	n/a	7063	n/a	25116	8.8
1982	22639	n/a	9665	n/a	32304	11.3
1983	22209	n/a	9514	n/a	31723	11.0
1984	21955	n/a	10366	n/a	32321	11.2
1985	23336	14.4	10680	7.7	34016	11.3
1986	23805	14.7	10700	7.7	34505	11.5
1987	25506	15.8	10796	8.0	36304	12.2
1988	22076	13.8	8998	6.5	31074	10.4
1989	18144	11.4	6531	4.6	24495	8.2
1990	14807	9.5	5007	3.4	19814	6.6
1991	17084	11.0	5278	3.6	22362	7.4

TABLE 1: 1987-BASED POPULATION PROJECTIONS 1987-2005

	1987	1995	2001	CHANGE 1987-2001
East Lothian	81,860	85,450	88,790	+9%
Edinburgh	438,720	435,730	432,830	– 1%
Midlothian	81,440	80,980	81,260	0
West Lothian	141,680	151,380	159,630	+13%
LOTHIAN	743,700	753,540	762,500	+3%

Source: Registrar General

TABLE 2: NUMBERS ECONOMICALLY ACTIVE LOTHIAN REGION 1988-2001

	1988	1995	2001
MALES			
Population 16+	287,500	290,800	292,600
Activity Rate	75.6	75.3	74.8
Economically Active	217,400	219,100	218,800
FEMALES			
Population 16+	318,600	317,000	316,100
Activity Rate	55.9	58.1	58.5
Economically Active	178,200	184,100	184,800
TOTAL LABOUR SUPPLY	395,500	403,200	403,600

Source: RG 1987-based population projection, DE Gazette, April 1989.

Yet there is proof that Edinburgh is breeding a new generation of local entrepreneurs. In the 1980s, the stock of VAT registered companies in Edinburgh rose by 28% (to nearly ten thousand). Tom Farmer came home from the USA imbued with an American customer service ethos and built his Kwik Fit tyre and exhaust replacement business into a European multinational. Angus Grossart created the first genuine Scottish merchant banking house on the back of North Sea oil, then went on to fund major movies such as *Chariots of Fire* and *Gandhi*. David Murray has built a conglomerate of property, North Sea engineering and media interests. In the cultural industries, David McWhinnie's La Mancha company makes and sells hundreds of hours of video documentaries to the world, and Bruce Findlay (former manager of U2) and impresario Pete Irvlne have made Edinburgh a major player in popular music.

THE FUTURE EDINBURGH'S AGENDA IN EUROPE

If the great city constantly reinvents itself, how will Edinburgh reinvent itself in the next generation? The answer lies in the city's response to the nature of European change. Post-Berlin Wall, Europe is evolving towards a single economic and political entity. But freed of the straitjacket of both the Yalta spheres of influence, and of the artificial boundaries of nation states invented in the smoke-filled rooms of Vienna or Versailles, the new Europe will be a Europe of resurgent regions and competing city states. Edinburgh's task is to rejoin this Europe of the regions and cities after a long detour of servicing the British Empire and defending itself from London centralism. And to do that, Edinburgh has to choose what its role will be in the new Europe.

Today Edinburgh is supremely placed to become the most influential city of a reborn Baltic Hanseatic League to act as a counterweight to the growing economic power of the Mediterranean and South Germany. Edinburgh's economic advantages are immense. She is the undisputed dominant financial centre of Northern Europe and could easily supply the necessary capital for both a free market Scandinavia and the new economies of St Petersburg or Gdansk. Edinburgh's first language is English, the only language common to all North Europe. To fulfil such a role Edinburgh requires not only the will but also the means. A new generation of communications infrastructure is needed, including a roll-on/roll-off passenger and freight sea terminal sited at Leith or Rosyth, and the expansion of a locally-controlled Edinburgh airport to take advantage of deregulated European air services to provide more direct flights to the Continent.

We might define the dilemma of Edinburgh's economic future thus: Edinburgh was the heart of the European Enlightenment - in other words, of rationalism and modernism. But the psyche of Edinburgh is also permeated with rank Scottish Calvinism and its attendant conservative values. These two sides of the city's character are permanently at war with each other. Edinburgh's future as a great city depends on which side gains the upper hand.

MANUFACTURING SECTOR EMPLOYMENT IN EDINBURGH

	Full-Time	Part-Time	Total	% of Manufacturing Employment
Chemical Industry	1600	300	1900	6
Mechanical Engineering	1700		1700	5
Electrical & Electronic Engineering	10000	200	10200	5
Food & Drink	7800	900	8700	26
Timber & Wooden Furniture	1100		1100	3
Paper, Printing & Publishing	4100	200	4300	13
Other Manufacturing	5000	300	5300	16
Total	31300	1900	33200	100

SERVICE SECTOR EMPLOYMENT IN EDINBURGH

	Full-Time	Part-Time	Total	% of Manufacturing Employment
Wholesale Distribution	7300	900	8200	4
Retail Distribution	12600	10500	23100	12
Hotel & Catering	7100	6600	13700	7
Transport	8900	500	9400	5
Post & Telecommunications	3000	100	3100	2
Financial Services	19200	2100	21300	11
Business Services	17700	3000	20700	11
Public Administration	18700	1100	19800	10
Education	15300	6700	22000	12
Health Services	11000	8000	19000	10
Other Services	18900	12300	31200	16
Total	139700	51800	191500	100

View of the Lawnmarket, Edinburgh. *William Gavin Herdman (City Art Centre, Edinburgh)*

A CITY
OF
CHARACTERS

GEORGE ROSIE

George Rosie is a freelance writer and broadcaster.
He was educated at Trinity Academy, Edinburgh and
the School of Architecture at Edinburgh College of Art.
He has contributed to a wide range of publications,
written and presented numerous award-winning
radio and television documentaries and was
the Scottish Affairs Correspondent of the
Sunday Times from 1976-1986.

'...Captain Edward
Topham found
Edinburgh raucous, dirty
and unsafe, rivalled only
by 18th century
Madrid for sheer
squalor'

The citizenry of Edinburgh have never lived up to their surroundings. Any summer visitor wading through the pizza dishes and Coke tins on Princes Street or Lothian Road knows that. In 1635 an English visitor (one Sir William Brereton) opined that *"This city is placed in a dainty healthful pure air, and doubtless were a most healthful place to live were not the inhabitants most sluttish, nasty and slothful people."* Another Englishman (the government spy Daniel Defoe) while admiring the beauty of the landscape felt that the *"nastiness of the place"* could not be gainsaid.

For his part Captain Edward Topham found Edinburgh raucous, dirty and unsafe, rivalled only by 18th-century Madrid for sheer squalor. As late as 1944 that redoubtable Chinese traveller and note-taker Chiang Yee discovered the denizens of ancient and elegant Auld Reekie to be almost alarmingly sociable (they kept trying to force whisky down his throat).

Maybe it is this startling contrast between the graciousness of the city and the gracelessness of the citizenry that has given Edinburgh its reputation for duality and shiftiness. Certainly it comes as no surprise that the world's best fable of the divided self was written by an Edinburgh man.

Edinburgh does seem to have the knack of producing Janus-faced characters. Even more sinister than Deacon Brodie was the figure of Major Weir, the 17th-century Presbyterian fanatic and preacher who confessed to devil worship and debauchery (and ended his days burnt at the city's stake). In the early 19th-century Edinburgh spawned Dr Robert Knox, that much-respected anatomist who was one of the fathers of modern racism and a customer of that murderous duo Burke and Hare. Burke himself was regarded as a *"respectable man"* - apart from the fact that he was a serial killer.

'I've lived in the city all my life. It has changed a lot. The level of service is superb and it's a great place to bring up kids'

BRIAN MACEWAN
MUSICIAN
(HIS DAUGHTER IS CALLED MANDY)

For centuries the Edinburgh mob was a byword for violence and unpredictability. Its leaders used to lay down the law to the city magistrates. In 1736 it hunted down the Captain of the Town Guard (the equivalent of the Chief Constable) and lynched him from a pole in the Grassmarket. And while the Chief Constable of Lothian and Borders Police can now sleep soundly in his bed, Edinburgh still has some of the hardest-pressed police offices in Britain. Football crowds, discos and late-night drinking have a way of erupting into the kind of violence that can take dozens of officers (and their dogs) to quell.

The social geography of Edinburgh seems to confirm the duality: Old Town, New Town; run-down late mediaeval tenements and neo-classical elegance; urban grandeur and the worst AIDS problem in Britain; the richest financial community outside London and grubby streets; douce churchgoers and thuggish football fans. Behind the orderly and amiable persona of Dr Jekyll stands the cold, hard glare of Edward Hyde.

But the metaphor can be stretched too far. All cities have their contradictions and paradoxes. Under the glittering towers of Manhattan lie the horrors of Harlem and the South Bronx. The Ganja-dens of Brixton are a short walk from the bucolic delights of Dulwich Village. Not all the arrondissements of Paris are as comely as the 16th. Even the douce little city of Bath which is a kind of neo-classical Edinburgh in miniature has a sorry record for terrorising foreign students and tourists.

The fact is, every city seems to have a role on the world stage. And if Glasgow's is (still and unfairly) that of an industrial ruin haunted by razor-slashing drunks, Edinburgh's is of a chilly place inhabited by variations on the theme of Miss Jean Brodie. A sniffish, cold-hearted kind of place, stalked by flinty lawyers and hard-eyed accountants. To Glaswegians, Edinburgh is all *fur coats and nae knickers*" as the old jibe goes. None of which Edinburgh folk recognise. It just makes them sigh with exasperation. It is, in fact, pretty hard to trace where the notion of Edinburgh's supposed hyper-respectability originates. Possibly it lies in the fact that Edinburgh houses Scotland's biggest middle-class population. Or perhaps, as Edinburgh people suspect, it is all just sour grapes on the part of Glaswegians and those other Scots who are fated (some would say doomed) to live outwith Edinburgh.

But there's no doubt that Edinburgh is one of Europe's more baffling cities. It has most of the trappings of a small European capital (Oslo, say, or Copenhagen) but none of the political clout. It may see itself as the centre of the Scottish universe, but to the English it is just another middle-ranking provincial centre, on a par with Newcastle or Bristol, perhaps, but not nearly as important as Birmingham or Manchester. As a stateless capital Edinburgh lives with a hole where its political heart used to be. The pseudo capital of a nearly country.

And yet at the same time, Edinburgh wields more power and influence than any British city outside of London. Enough, it seems, to keep the city's élites well paid, happy, and thirled to the status quo. The Scottish parliament may have

Dr. Robert Knox *(Edinburgh Central Library)*
Inset: Burke the murderer (City Art Centre, Edinburgh)

'We rode
to Edinburgh;
one of the dirtiest
cities I have ever
seen not excepting
Cologne in
Germany'

JOHN WESLEY

'There is a sense of space around the city. The set, the hills the buildings are all tremendous assets. It's a lovely city to work in'

MIKE LAXTON
CIVIL SERVANT

'I came from Sri Lanka to go to university in Edinburgh. I feel it is a good place to study. I especially like the people in Edinburgh, although it took a while to pick up the accent!'

SAPUMAL PIHILLEGEDERA
ACCOUNTING STUDENT
NAPIER UNIVERSITY

Mr Brodie. *J. Kay*
(City Art Centre, Edinburgh)

'I'm not really keen on cities, but I like it here. Edinburgh is a greener city'

PAUL FARRELL
OUTDOOR INSTRUCTOR

The execution of Deacon Brodie. *Alexander Ritchie (City Art Centre, Edinburgh)*

long gone, but Edinburgh remains the centre of Scotland's legal system. In criminal cases at least, Edinburgh's decision is final. There is no appeal to the House of Lords.

Edinburgh is also the ecclesiastical heart of Scotland. It is home to the Church of Scotland ("*by law established*") whose General Assembly floods the city with Presbyterian ministers every May. The Free Church of Scotland (one of the Kirk's many offspring) is also based in Edinburgh, although its strength lies in the Highlands and Islands.

Her Majesty's Government operates in Scotland largely (but not entirely) through the Edinburgh-based Scottish Office, whose 13,000 or so civil servants administer London's diktat. Its head, the Secretary of State for Scotland, is a member of the British Cabinet. Fittingly, perhaps, his role is dual. He is both Scotland's man in London and London's man in Scotland.

None of which does anything to alleviate the pain of those parts of the intelligentsia who seek home rule or an independent Scotland. They see in these Edinburgh-rooted institutions the mummified corpse of a nation which needs only an elected parliament to galvanise it into life. But they also know that whether or not the corpse stirs depends on the hyper-cautious voters of the rural areas and the hard-case Socialists of Glasgow and its environs. And many of them are deeply suspicious of what they see as Edinburgh's ambitions.

But even the most unionist of the Edimbourgeois tend to be touchy about their role as guardians of Scotland's historic capital. English visitors are often taken aback by the ferocity with which apparently genteel Scots will defend Edinburgh's status. The idea of Edinburgh being a "real" capital, like London or Paris or Washington strikes them as absurd, even a bit pathetic. Edinburgh is just enough of a capital to nurse its own self-importance, but not enough of a capital to impress anybody else. As ever, ambiguity and ambivalence prevail.

This feeling of unfulfilled potential haunts the city's mental landscape. It infuriates and saddens. The poet Hugh MacDiarmid summed it up brilliantly when he wrote "*there is no one really alive in Edinburgh yet, they are all living at the tiniest fraction of the life they could easily have*". MacDiarmid saw Edinburgh's citizens as people living in great houses "*who prefer to live in their cellar and keep all the rest sealed up*".

Edinburgh's reputation for Presbyterian piety is more easily explained; the city has more churches per head of population than any city in Britain. The skyline of modern Edinburgh is heavily spiked with ecclesiastical spires and towers. But this is not, as many seem to think, because Edinburgh folk are a religious breed. It is a consequence of the great Disruption of 1843 when almost half the congregations of the established Church of Scotland marched out to form the Free Church. In the process, they doubled the number of churches in the city (and in the rest of Scotland).

In Edinburgh nothing is ever quite what it seems. Even the southern suburbs, which seem to epitomise "respectable" Edinburgh are full of surprises. Ronald Searle's famous centre of mayhem and chaos, St Trinian's School for Young Ladies was (loosely) modelled on St. Trinnean's School for Girls in Marchmont. The school was run by Miss C. Fraser Lee along the liberal 'Dalton' lines, which in stuffy circles was regarded as sheer anarchy. Searle learned all about St. Trinnean's when he was posted to Edinburgh as an army engineer in 1941. He found the conjunction of genteel young ladies wreaking chaos irresistible. The rest, as they say, is history.

Even Miss Jean Brodie, the fictional schoolteacher now seen as the very essence of Edinburgh respectability, is not what she seems. Her creator Muriel Spark makes it plain that Miss Brodie and her ilk were no caricatures, but women of real complexity. "*There were legions of her kind during the 1930s,*" she wrote, "*women from the age of thirty and upward who crowded their war-bereaved spinsterhood with voyages of discovery into new ideas and energetic practices in art, social welfare, education or religion.*" Italian Fascism - which was Jean Brodie's predeliction - was just such a 'new idea'.

The Orkney-born poet Edwin Muir once observed that '*although Edinburgh is Scottish in itself, one cannot feel that the people who live in it are Scottish in any radical sense, or have any essential connection with it . . .*' Although he (probably) exaggerates, there is something in what Muir says. Edinburgh may be the historic heart of Scotland, but it is also one of the most Anglicised parts. Ever since the Union of the Crowns in 1603 the Scots aristocracy and gentry and their myriad hangers-on have been taking their social and political cues from England (or, to be more precise, London).

The result has been the "Englishing" of Scottish high society. Upper-class Scots almost invariably speak with English accents, worship in Anglican

'Edinburgh people have a veneer of reserve. Underneath they are extremely nice - that makes it for me'

GEORGE KERR
TAXI DRIVER
(CAB VICTOR 150)

'I had wanted to move to Edinburgh for years. In 1989 we made the move and I enjoy everything about living here'

EILEEN DURWARD
MEMBER, WORKERS' CO-OP
SEEDS CAFE

churches, and send their children to English schools and universities. They may deck themselves out in tartan and dance a mean eightsome reel, but they disdain the Scotland in which most of their compatriots live. That syndrome shows little signs of abating. As a result, Edinburgh abounds with English-style private schools to cater for the gentry and their admirers. Edinburgh has for long been notorious for its hierarchy of schools; "public" schools like Fettes College, Loretto School and Merchiston Castle at the top, local authority comprehensives at the bottom with the fee-paying like Edinburgh Academy, George Heriot's and George Watson's in

SOME LORD PROVOSTS OF EDINBURGH WHO MADE THEIR MARK

The Rt. Hon. Norman Irons

One of my predecessors as Lord Provost was flung into the Tower of London and put on trial because he happened to support the wrong political party. Another, who was obviously not popular in his native city, was physically attacked more than once. A third was assassinated – the only Lord Provost of Edinburgh to have suffered such a fate - so far. These bald facts, while true, give a misleading impression of the risks of this historic office, which I now have the honour to occupy.

There are indeed risks in being Lord Provost in modern times, but these days the occupant is more

diplomat than warrior. The time has gone when the job called more for the qualities of military governor than civil administrator.

To read the history of the office of Lord Provost, which spans 700 years, is to study the story of Scotland itself for much of our national drama was enacted in the streets and closes of Edinburgh, the ancient capital of a sovereign nation. The story is one of turbulence and bloodshed, and yet it is also inspirational and marked by many notable achievements.

The office of Lord Provost can be traced back to 1296, though the records during the two centuries after that are far from complete. The most famous soldier in our ranks was Sir William Kirkcaldy of Grange, who in the sixteenth century was also captain of Edinburgh Castle. At the end of a famous siege by an English army, having been obliged to surrender, Kirkcaldy was handed over to his fellow Scots. The contemporary political situation, unfortunately, led to Kirkcaldy's execution, and his head was displayed on the Castle wall. But strictly speaking, Kirkcaldy was not Lord Provost at the time, having been replaced the year before.

Civil disorder was almost a fact of life. The vehemence of the Edinburgh mob was notorious and it

features prominently in any account of riot and tumult in the Old Town. In 1561, for example, the craft apprentices went on the rampage because the Town Council had banned the holding of their May Day sports. The upshot was that the Lord Provost and the Council were besieged in the Tollbooth, and the riot was only ended by the intervention of troops sent down from the Castle.

However, that was only a "little local difficulty", compared with the repercussions in London over the Porteous Riots of 1736. When the mob dragged Captain Porteous, commander of the Town Guard, from the Tollbooth and lynched him in the Grassmarket from a barber's pole, Queen Caroline and the Government in London were furious. The general view was that the magistrates had been intimidated by the rioters, proving reluctant to order the military to suppress the violent disorder. Provost Alexander Wilson was summoned to London, where he was promptly imprisoned and not admitted to bail for three weeks. All sorts of threats were made against Edinburgh itself.

In the ranks of Lord Provosts the outstanding figure of all time must be George Drummond, if only because he was elected to the office six times in the space of 12 years. He

between. Just as an Englishman is reputed to be able to instantly "place" another Englishman by his accent, so the Edimbourgeois can rank one another socially by their almae mater. This can and frequently does induce the kind of social/scholastic neurosis familiar in England but virtually unknown elsewhere in Scotland.

Yet even a confused pseudo capital like Edinburgh has its attractions. All through the 18th, 19th and into the 20th centuries, gifted Scots swarmed into Edinburgh to add their talents to those of the natives. The results were dazzling. The city was home to scientists, philosophers, artists, divines and litterateurs. It has

'You've just got to go into town and you've got the whole of Europe sitting at your feet'

PAUL CARTER
ART STUDENT

'I grew up in Edinburgh. When I'm away I always think about coming back'

MRS PEARMAIN
RESIDENT

'Edinburgh's great! Everything is very central. I'd like to settle here'

JIM BROWN
UNEMPLOYED

was obviously a towering influence in eighteenth century Edinburgh. His outstanding memorial is the Georgian New Town, which was born thanks to his vision. The value of the New Town to Europe's architectural heritage, and the sterling work that has been done during the past two decades to conserve it, was recognised in 1987 with the award of the Europa Nostra Medal of Honour.

Drummond was also a leader in such projects as the building of the Royal Exchange (now the City Chambers), the draining of the Nor' Loch, construction of the North Bridge and founding of the Royal Infirmary.

One of my favourite stories from the Victorian period concerns the unfortunate Sir James Forrest. When Queen Victoria and the Prince Consort visited the city the plan was that the Lord Provost and the other magistrates should meet the royal procession at Inverleith in order to present the keys of the city. Alas, for some reason the civic party was late and missed the rendezvous. Queen Victoria was not amused and pressed on, leaving the embarrassed dignitaries to do a U-turn and try to catch up.

The only Englishman ever to hold the office of Lord Provost was Sir James Falshaw, a Yorkshireman. He was a civil engineer who had moved to Scotland during the period of construction of the railways.

In the present century, a number of names stand out. The first of these is Sir Will Y. Darling, a charismatic character of great zest and enthusiasm who was eminently suited to this office in the depths of the Second World War. Will Y. Darling invariably wore a top hat, a custom which, even then, was regarded as a bit old-fashioned. The riveting fact was that he always wore the top hat pushed back on his bald head. This gave him the undeniable air of a showman, which he breezily conceded he was. But he got things done.

Sir James Miller is unique as the only Lord Provost who went on to become Lord Mayor of London, and my immediate predecessor, Eleanor McLaughlin, was also unique, making history in 1988 by becoming the first woman to occupy the office of Lord Provost of Edinburgh. I am the first Nationalist to become Lord Provost.

The final name is that of Sir John Falconer, who will always be thought of as one of the founding fathers of the Edinburgh Festival first held in 1947. Since then it has grown to be the world's biggest arts festival, with incalculable benefits not only to Edinburgh but also to the rest of the world.

Cardinal Beaton's House, Cowgate
John Le Conte (City Art Centre, Edinburgh)

Edinburgh Characters. *E. Holt*
(Edinburgh Central Library)

produced world-class sportsmen like Eric Liddell, Allan Wells, Ken Buchanan, Dougal Haston and actors and entertainers like Harry Lauder, Alistair Sim, Ronnie Corbett, Lindsay Kemp and Sean Connery (Britain's only "bankable" superstar).

And while it is centuries since Edinburgh was a hotbed of sedition and/or insurrection, the city has produced its share of hard-line politicians. One was the extreme Protestant John Cormack, whose anti-Catholic 'Protestant Action' movement plagued the city all through the 1930s. And Edinburgh spawned one of the hero-martyrs of the 1916 Easter Rising in Dublin, the revolutionary socialist James Connolly, who was executed by the British army after the abortive uprising. Connolly was a Scot, born in the dismal Cowgate district of the Old Town, the son of poor Irish immigrants.

Like most European cities, Edinburgh's social texture has been enriched by immigration. Edinburgh is no cultural monolith and there is an overlay of "ethnic" groups throughout Edinburgh, some of whom have been in the city for generations.

The truth is the character of Edinburgh, like the character of most European cities, is an intricate (even bewildering) tapestry of subcultures, interests and traditions. Many of them have little in common. It is hard to see the community of interest between a Court of Session judge and a Gorgie slaughterhouse worker. Or a Charlotte Square currency dealer and a Fountainbridge brewery hand. Or a New Town antique dealer and a deckhand on the sewage barge *Gardyloo*. Or one of the barons of the life assurance industry and a drug-wrecked youth crouching in a hovel in a peripheral housing estate.

In one of his finest essays Robert Louis Stevenson describes leaning over the rail of the North Bridge and watching the trains trundle out of Waverley

CHILD FRIENDLY EDINBURGH

Isabel Wilshaw

Edinburgh is a giant adventure playground. What other city in the world can boast an extinct volcano in its midst? Add to that a castle with ramparts and cannons, an Old Town where every close hides an exciting story, a wonderful variety of green spaces, swimming pools, museums and galleries, and the longest artificial ski slope in Europe. A child could have a different adventure every day of the week.

In 1991 Edinburgh declared its intention to become the first Child Friendly City in the United Kingdom, an ambitious idea enthusiastically backed by the local authorities and the business community. The Lord Provost of Edinburgh, Eleanor McLaughlin, launched a campaign backed by Edinburgh District Council and the Chamber of Commerce to alert businesses and recreation centres to the benefits of being Child Friendly - more customers! Many shops, hotels and restaurants, swimming pools and libraries now display our sticker which says "We Care about Kids". Marks and Spencer made a point of listening to parents and as a result installed automatic doors and moved their children's department to ground level. The Bridge Inn has been nominated

Station en route to brighter skies. He writes: *'Happy the passengers who shake off the dust of Edinburgh and have heard for the last time the cry of the east wind among her chimney-tops! And yet the place establishes an interest in people's hearts; go where they will, they find no city of the same distinction; go where they will, they take pride in their old home.'*

It was a sentiment that Stevenson lived. He died in the sunshine of Samoa while working on *Weir of Hermiston,* that sour tale of a grim Edinburgh judge. Under the blue Pacific sky his imagination was haunting the old sandstone of Parliament Close, and the dingy corridors of the High Court of Justice. Among the smiling Polynesians he saw the pinched faces he knew from the Scottish bar. In the mellifluous music of the islanders he heard the intricate arguments of Scots law.

The man, it seems, could be removed from the city, but never the city from the man. Edinburgh has that effect.

'East, West hame's best and Edinburgh's the best city in the world'

*GRAHAM BRODIE
STUDENT
STEVENSON COLLEGE*

'I married a girl from Edinburgh and we ended up living here. I enjoy the easy pace of life'

*JOHN HAYNES
RETIRED ENGLAND AND FULHAM
FOOTBALLER (THE DOG IS CALLED EMMA)*

UK Children's Caterer of the Year.

Edinburgh Vision compiled a list of Child Friendly hotels and guest houses, Edinburgh District Council published their *Child Friendly Guide to Edinburgh*, available free of charge and featuring places nominated by children - the demand for it is huge from residents and visitors alike. Lothian Regional Council published its *Children and Family Charter*, which spells out to every child in Lothian his or her entitlement to be heard and respected.

The central aim of Child Friendly Edinburgh is to make Edinburgh a good place to grow up in. If it is a good city for children, who are its most vulnerable citizens and its future, then it will be a good city for everyone. The challenge now is to shift the attitudes of planners, traffic engineers, architects and many others to consider children's priorities as central, and not an added extra. We have made a start. Child Friendly Edinburgh is part of our civic vocabulary now.

We will build on that commitment to ensure that Edinburgh gives strong messages to its children that they are valued members of our city.

*Leanne Horsburg, Primary 7
Sighthill Primary School*

*'Fairwell,
Edina!
Pleasing name, -
Congenial to
my heart!'*

THOMAS CAMPBELL

CONTRIBUTORS

are listed on their title pages, except for the following:-

THE RT. HON. NORMAN IRONS
Lord Provost of Edinburgh

The Rt. Hon. Norman Irons, C.Eng, MIMEchE, JP was elected Lord Provost of Edinburgh on 12 May 1992.
A member of the Scottish National Party since 1973 he was elected Councillor for the Drumbrae Ward in January 1976 and has represented an area of Corstorphine since then. The Lord Provost was born in Glasgow but has spent most of his life in Edinburgh, being educated at George Heriot's School before attending colleges in Edinburgh and London. Aged 51 he is a Chartered Mechanical Engineer and is married with two children. The Lord Provost's principal recreation is rugby and he is President of Lismore RFC.

ERIC MILLIGAN
Councillor, Convenor Lothian Region

Born in Edinburgh in 1951, Eric Milligan was elected as a Labour Party councillor to Edinburgh District Council in 1974. In 1978 he travelled up the city's Royal Mile to Lothian Regional Council. He first became Chairman of the Finance Committee at the age of 29 and has been the Council's Convenor since 1990. A former President of the Convention of Scottish Local Authorities, he is well known throughout Scotland. Outside politics, Eric enjoys a prominent role in the arts and is an enthusiastic football supporter.

GORDON GREENHILL

Gordon Greenhill is a section head with the City of Edinburgh District Council's Environmental Health Department. He is responsible for the section which assesses the environmental impact of new developments within the city.
He was involved in the drawing up of Edinburgh's Environmental Action Plan and Pollution Monitoring Programming and is he on the Co-ordinating Committee of the Festival of the Environment.

CHARLES WINTER, CBE
President of the Edinburgh Chamber of Commerce and Manufacturers

One of the best known of Scottish businessmen, Charles Winter has had a lengthy career with the Royal Bank of Scotland, from a clerk behind the counter in 1949 to Chief Executive and today Vice-Chairman of Scotland's most internationally-minded bank. His work has brought him into contact with a wide range of businesses not only in Edinburgh and the rest of Scotland, but also in England, North America and continental Europe.

SUDHEER CARROLL

Sudheer Carroll was born in 1934. He studied at the University of London under the late Prof. Pearsall, a pioneer of modern plant ecology. In 1957 he moved to Wales and obtained an MSc for research on agricultural grasses. From 1967 he worked at an Edinburgh research institute breeding primitive potatoes from Colombia and Peru. He joined the Edinburgh Wildlife Group as Education Officer in 1989 and has since worked with many local schools and community organisations on wildlife and conservation issues.

MHAIRI MacKENZIE-ROBINSON
Administrator, Edinburgh Festival Fringe

Mhairi MacKenzie-Robinson was born 33 years ago and educated in Scotland. After five years away, and a degree in psychology from Durham University, she returned to Edinburgh. Temporary jobs with the Fringe Society and other Festival work over previous summers led to a full-time appointment as Assistant Administrator in 1982. In 1986 she became the first female Administrator of the Fringe. She continues to enjoy spreading the word about the history and work of the Fringe, and the role it plays in the arts today.

ISABEL WILSHAW

Isabel Wilshaw studied languages at Edinburgh University and has worked in secondary, adult and higher education. She later worked in the voluntary sector managing media training programmes for the unemployed, in partnership with the BBC. As Director of Edinburgh Vision she brings people together to make things happen for Edinburgh. She is committed to improving the quality of communication, and is putting her linguistic skills to good use now interpreting between accountants and doctors, businessmen and community workers. Isabel has three children who are particularly pleased that their mum has been instrumental in setting up the "Child Friendly Edinburgh" campaign.

LAURA FIORENTINI

Laura Fiorentini was born in Genoa. After working for some years at the British Consulate in Milan, she came to Scotland in 1980 and settled in Edinburgh. Following a spell as secretary of the Italian Institute of Culture, she is now working for the Italian Consulate in Edinburgh. Since 1986, she has also been Honorary Secretary of the Scottish Centre of PEN, the international association of writers.

WERNER KITTEL

German-born Werner Kittel lives in Edinburgh's New Town from where he works as a freelance interpreter and translator. He recently spent two years with VSO in Indonesia, where he taught English at Bandung University. His interests include playing squash, running and hillwalking.

FAMOUS FREEMEN OF THE CITY

Daily Record

Sean Connery

Sir Walter Scott,
Sir Henry Raeburn

J. M. Barrie,
*Sir William
Nicholson*

David Livingstone,
Thomas Annan

*Scottish National
Portrait Gallery*

Andrew Carnegie,
Catherine Ouless

W hat do Giuseppe Garibaldi, Samuel Pepys, Benjamin Franklin, the Queen Mother, Yehudi Menuhin and Sean Connery have in common?

That could be an obscure question from "Trivial Pursuit" but in fact it is a question that should be answered quickly by any Edinburgh councillor or local historian. Because all of the above - and many more distinguished names from Benjamin Disraeli to Earl Mountbatten of Burma - were or are Freemen of the City of Edinburgh.

Sean Connery is the most recent name added to the list. The "Freedom of the City" was conferred on him in a magnificent ceremony in the Usher Hall on the 11th of June 1991 to "*celebrate his distinguished contribution to world cinema; to mark his largely unpublicised work in founding the Scottish International Education Trust, whose aims include the promotion of new Scottish talent; and in particular to recognise the respect and high esteem in which he is held by the people of the City of Edinburgh*".

The office of Freeman is an ancient one which was originally not an honour, but a necessity. Until about 150 years ago anyone who wanted to work within the city boundaries as a craftsman or merchant had to agree, in return for the privilege, to take on duties guarding and governing the burgh. This was called becoming a burgess, and the Freedom Scroll that is now presented was originally called the burgess ticket.

For over 500 years the city has also created Honorary Freemen. The first was Sir Edward Boncle, Provost of the newly founded Trinity College, who was given the burgess ticket in 1459 in gratitude for his aid and counsel.

As time has passed the scope of the honour has been widened to include not just those who have contributed something to the city itself, but also those who have contributed to the nation and the world. Such Freemen in past centuries have included David Livingstone, Ulysses S. Grant, David Lloyd George, Sir Harry Lauder, Winston Churchill and King Olav of Norway.

The list includes prime ministers, monarchs, soldiers and statesmen, writers, inventors, entertainers and many others. Once the Freedom of the City included privileges such as the grazing of sheep on the Meadows. It meant that an individual had joined the society of his peers and could be relied on to protect and nurture the city to which he belonged.

Now the Freedom of the City confers something even more valuable. It means that the freeman or freewoman has earned not just a place amongst the people of Edinburgh, but the ultimate place of respect, honour and - being Edinburgh - affection.

Sean Connery deserves no less from his former fellow citizens. And neither do the others in the long list of fame.